enough to entice even the most reticent of victims to risk emerging into healing."

—**Roxanne George, Ph.D., LMFT**,
Acacia Rising Counseling

"I commend your vulnerability and strength in sharing your story. Your book is so powerful and moving that I had to take my time reading it, hence the delay in responding to you. I was especially taken by the way you survived your traumatic years and your later journey of the way you made sense of the unjust, and horrendous acts. This is pure strength and resiliency!... Congratulations on your journey to set yourself free because the one thing that no one could or can take away from you is your right to deserve peace, hope and happiness...It has been an honor reading your story, thank you for sharing this with me."

—**Antoinette Gupta, MS LMFT**

"*Even the Trees Were Crying* is a book of hope and healing for male and female survivors of sexual abuse or SA. The author, Ernie Carwile, bravely shares his own deeply personal story of SA in hopes that others may recover from their "soul stealing" experiences. Startling statistics throughout the book grab the reader's attention and help them to know that they are not alone. Carwile relates his inspirational journey recovering from trauma and highlights a turning point with the healing powers of EMDR (Eye Movement Desensitization and Reprocessing) Therapy. This book provides hope for survivors and gives them "steps for healing," so that their suffering can stop and real recovery can begin. A helpful book for survivors, EMDR therapists, and other helping professionals."

—**Lemecia Lindsey**, LICSW Certified EMDR Therapist and EMDR Consultant, Vancouver EMDR Therapy in Washington

"Thank you for allowing me to read your book, it was riveting and inspiring! I found this work on sexual abuse and healing through EMDR to be a testament to the strength of the human spirit and the amazing work that can be accomplished through EMDR!"

—**T.J. Stanfield, MA, LPC**, Approved EMDR Consultant

"I just finished your book and all I can say is: Amazing. That was such an experience for me. You have been to those dark alleys and know what you are talking about. I really liked how you explained and uncovered what grooming looks like. I loved how you related your experience to trials in general that everyone must go through. This was a very intense read...with a positive end."

—**Darren Gillespie**, EMDR Therapist

"A hopeful account of the courageous journey of recovery from the pain of childhood sexual abuse, told from a man's perspective, with a good basic understanding of the role of EMDR and other forms of

Endorsements and Praise

for

*Even The Trees Were Crying*

"I invested [time] in you because I believe in your book. And you are an inspiration...You are an amazing human being who managed to stay alive through the darkness and in so doing, found healing and light...A very powerful message to those still in the darkness and to those of us who have a calling to help traumatized people to heal."

**—Nancy Newport**, LPC, LMFT

"Carwile's book addresses an important topic and is a helpful read for people who have suffered from sexual abuse and the traumatic 'fall out' or symptoms that result from this type of trauma. Recovery is possible, reading this hopeful book helps you see how."

**—Hope Payson LCSW**, LADC, Licensed Clinical Social Worker, Licensed Alcohol and Drug Counselor, EMDRIA Approved Consultant

"Ernie Carwile's memoir is an empathic, sensitive, and knowledgeable guide for anyone struggling to recover from SA. Both client and therapist will have an encouraging and intimate companion on their healing journey with Mr. Carwile's book by their side. Highly recommended."

**—Elizabeth Belkin, LCSW**, EMDR Consultant

"Ernie Carwile shares his personal experience with abuse in a thoughtful, compelling way. He validates symptoms and frustrations shared by victims while offering hope to those who continue to suffer. Readers who have experienced abuse themselves will easily connect with the kindness with which Ernie expresses himself and with his journey of hope and healing."

—**Lee Ann Durfey**, EMDR Therapist

"I am very grateful to have read this book. It is a heartbreaking story, but one that gives so much hope to trauma survivors. As an EMDR Certified Therapist, I believe deeply in the healing that EMDR therapy can provide. This book is proof that you can survive and heal from severe trauma and that EMDR therapy works!"

—**Angie Ridings, LPC, LADC, CSAT, CMAT**, EMDR Certified Therapist

"Your story is one that inspires hope and that is missing for so many "victims" of sexual abuse...and a key to healing."

—**Beth Alyson Troy Maris**, EMDR Therapist

"*Even the Trees Were Crying* is an excellent starting point for both survivors of sexual abuse, and those who want to understand more about sexual abuse. Ernie Carwile has managed to beautifully weave a lifetime of trauma and healing into a book that is short enough to read in one sitting, yet powerful therapy. I hope it inspires others to take this journey and find the recovery approaches that work for them."

**—Pamela Rogers, MA, LPCC,**
EMDRIA Certified Consultant

"Ernie Carwile's *Even the Trees Were Crying* is written in the most authentic and honest way. He shares the horrors of sexual abuse in a way that releases shame and guilt and safely guides the reader in how to bring their own dark experiences into the light where truth and healing can be found. He offers both emotional and practical ways to heal from the residual traumatic effects of sexual abuse so that the reader doesn't have to feel so alone. I want to encourage anyone picking up this book to allow Ernie Carwile to join you on your journey of healing and know that health and freedom are in your future."

**—Lesley Goth PsyD**, Trauma specialist,
Broomfield Colorado

"Ernie Carwile presents a courageously personal and moving portrayal of his journey from the pain of childhood sexual abuse into health and well-being. Ernie shares his healing experience with EMDR therapy from a non-clinical perspective, offering hope and encouragement to those who are suffering from the effects of trauma. As a clinician I can also attest to the potential for EMDR therapy to transform lives for the better."

**—Charlotte Winters, PhD**, EMDR Therapist
and Consultant in Newport Beach, CA

"Ernie, your book is a must read for society to begin to take down the heavy drapes that corrupt our vision and bury our hearts. Your book shines a light on the strength love and hope even through the most devastating acts that exist in this world... You shared the story of the Michael Jackson and the collective blind eye of society—this is a very powerful example of what happens in families and I hope one day we all break free from what we think is true and want to believe is true to what is actually true/possible."

**—April Minjarez**, EMDR Therapist

"Ernie Carwile's *Even the Trees Were Crying* is a powerful evocation of the plight of a sexually abused child. It details the psychological damage that these childhood experiences can have for the survivor's entire life, if not treated with EMDR or some equivalently effective therapy. It is also an inspiring memoir that demonstrates how with courage, support, and good therapy the survivor can regain a full and joyful life...Good luck with this effort. The country is in denial about this problem which was complicated by the period when therapists were encouraging false memories (satanic cults, etc.). It is important to make it safe for survivors to face the truth and be able to talk about it. I think this book could be a real help in that."

**—Lewis Engel, PhD**, Clinical Psychologist, EMDRIA Approved Consultant, Author of *Imaginary Crimes, Why We Punish Ourselves and How to Stop*, Houghton Mifflin, 1990

"Your frank writing and getting to the heart of your story was saddening but uplifting. The truthfulness of what you went through and the paths your life lead you on will be helpful to many people. It is difficult to find a book about sexual abuse that is frank, truthful and concise."

—**Tara Hast, LMFT**, EMDR Therapist

"A thoughtful exploration of the impact of sexual abuse from the inside. This book may be of benefit to the lay public, the thoughtful clinician, as well as to the person in recovery from their own abuse experiences."

—**Paul Callister**, Clinical Mental Health Counselor, EMDR Certified Therapist

"This book is truly a gift from one soul who has suffered severe traumatic abuse and healed; representing hope to others still on the journey. Carwile explains how he discovered a breakthrough therapy called EMDR (Eye Movement Desensitization and Reprocessing) as the most effective life transforming therapy for overcoming PTSD in its many forms...I wholeheartedly recommend this book."

—**Dr. Mel Rabin**, Licensed Clinical Psychologist, former faculty at Harvard Medical School, Clinical Training Staff at the EMDR Institute

"One of the most poignant and heartrending stories of the atrocities that sexual abuse and incest renders in the lives of its survivors. It is a story of courage, determination and fortitude that rends the veil of secrecy for men and creates hope that healing and restoration is possible."

**—Wanda K. Holloway, PsyD, LPC, LCSW**, EMDR Certified and Approved Consultant

"Ernie Carwile's words had me in tears after the first chapter. His story is not only heart wrenching, but truly shows the lifelong pain that sexual abuse victims suffer, as well as successful treatment modalities to heal from the emotional scars. Ernie's story can help other sexual abuse survivors heal from their past."

**—Erica Hough, MA, LPCC**, EMDR Certified Therapist, Laverne Counseling, Laverne, MN.

"As a therapist and combat veteran who regularly works with those struggling with PTSD, Ernie has accurately capture the battle survivors of sexual assault must face if they are hoping to find health and meaning in life. It is clear he found both in his story."

**—Christopher Floro, MA, LMFT**, AAMFT Approved Supervisor, EMDR Approved Consultant

"Ernie Carwile's book is an inspiring story of healing and growth that can provide hope and direction for anyone impacted by the terrible effects of sexual abuse. Through self-reflection, perseverance, and EMDR therapy, the author shows that anyone can overcome long-standing pain and find a renewed sense of purpose and zest for life.

—**Brittney Baxter Dameron**, LISW Therapist,
Southwest Iowa Families, Inc.

# Even The Trees
# Were Crying

Ernie Carwile

# Even The Trees Were Crying

Ernie Carwile

Verbena Pond Publishing Co., LLC

Copyright © 2017

All rights are reserved.

ISBN: 978-0-9987739-0-2

Library of Congress Control Number: 2017903286

Printed in the United States

# DEDICATION

---

*This book is dedicated to my father.*
*After doing everything you possibly could*
*to destroy me...I'm still here!*

# ACKNOWLEDGMENTS

Two people clearly stand out for their vital help in putting this book together. The first accolade is for my wife, friend and insightful critic, my Mary.

Secondly, my great appreciation to Ross Miller for his expertise in the details.

## Other Books by Ernie Carwile

---

*Crème de la Creme*

*The Magic of Creativity*

*And the Animals Shall Teach Us:*
*Angels in Disguise*

*Attitude: It's Not What You See,*
*It's How You See*

*Connected By The Soul:*
*Oh, The Oneness of Us All*

*Reclaiming the Power of Silence*

*Persistence: The Art of Failing*
*Until You Succeed*

*Where Do We Go From Here?*
*Death, The Next Great Adventure*

*Never Good Enough: Discover the*
*Treasure of Self-Acceptance*

*Chipped But Not Broken 2:*
*When Adversity Enhances The Human Spirit*

*The Storyteller 1*

A Few of the Many Endorsements /Thank yous

for the

Maxwell Winston Stone Series

"I would like to take this opportunity to thank you for sending me *Attitude: It's Not What You See, It's How You See*...I wish you all of the best in your future endeavors."

—Barack Obama
President of the United States

"Thank you very much for your book...It was 100% good stuff that we all need to absorb and live with."

—Steve Spurrier
Head Football Coach
University of South Carolina

"Some of the most spiritual yet realistic books of our time—they are phenomenal."

—Dr. Robert Carrol

"I have always taught my children to look on the bright side of life—and your book on attitude expresses this concept perfectly."

—Bill Owens
Governor of Colorado 1999–2007

"These books speak to the world. Everyone should read them."

—Edwin Alexander
Former Director of the Federal Home Loan Bank

"Thank you for your book on ATTITUDE. I'm adding it to my personal lending library at my office so my staff and others can read it, too."

—Governor Jennifer M. Granholm
State of Michigan

"There must be something BIGGER than the universe to brag about how much I enjoyed you and your books... How special they are and have definitely made a difference in my life."

—Debbie Wilden
President/CEO Cottonwood Chamber of Commerce, AZ

"Your works are very inspirational and provide the readers with gems of wisdom on how to pursue a more positive and harmonious life. They are truly remarkable."

—Governor Anibal Acevedo Vila
Commonwealth of Puerto Rico

# TABLE OF CONTENTS

*God must be very wise and strong to give humans*
*the free will to commit their atrocities on one*
*another ... I could never be God; I mean,*
*I would never give them that much freedom.*

—Internal dialogue

# BOOK 1

# THE INSIDIOUSNESS OF SEXUAL ABUSE

# ATTENTION:

*Beware that some of the content you are about to read could be triggering to sexual abuse survivors.*

# THE BEGINNING

OFFUTT AIR FORCE BASE
OMAHA, NEBRASKA
BASE HOUSING
CIRCA 1954

*I remember being five or six and awakening from another wrenching nightmare. The dream's setting was bright, fiery red with the devil present. My first thought was that I must have again forgotten to say my prayers before I went to sleep and this was my presumed, regular punishment for not doing so. Both my pajamas and my trusty sock-monkey were drenched in sweat from the torrid dream, yet*

*I gripped the sodden stuffed animal as if I could absorb a bit of comfort from it.*

*Normally, the darkness in my small bedroom didn't frighten me—except during nights like this. I strained to hear every little noise in the house dreading that I might hear the cracking and popping of his knees as he walked towards my room. I lay deathly still, barely breathing, sometimes holding my breath; hoping, hoping, hoping ... until, as my dark fears were realized, my bedroom door opened.*

*I initially squeezed my eyes tightly shut in the hope that this time was only another nightmare ... until the sickening touch of his hand on my body evaporated any such luck. Turning on the light so he could see me better, he turned my little body over onto my stomach before, all at the same time, pulling my pajama bottom and underpants down.*

*Entering me from behind, he whispered for me to be quiet as his hand covered my mouth, assuring my silence. The first thrust always shocked me; how painful it could be every time.*

*After a while, the pain diminished—or I became numb—and there were times he removed his hand from my mouth. Then I could only concentrate on* the reverberating slapping sound made from his thighs repetitively hitting against my small bottom. I wondered, if he was so concerned about being silent, why did he never concern himself with the loud noise this made? Couldn't anyone else hear it?

Oddly enough, this particular time an unusual thought entered my mind. For the first time, I looked back over my shoulder to see his facial expression. I was curious. What could he have been thinking while hurting me—his own son—so badly?

What I saw confused me even more. He was grimacing as if in pain, then anger, and soon rage dominated his face. It was as if he was mad at me. I also noticed that his eyes were shut tight—like mine had been at first.

I couldn't understand this. How could he be upset with me? Why was he punishing me when all I had been doing was sleeping in my bed? I tried to remember if I had done anything bad during the day but came up with nothing.

Finally finishing with me, he yanked up my underwear and pajamas and silently walked away as I lay silently whimpering, filled with guilt. My young mind reasoned that, somehow, I must have *been the cause of what happened, that for some unknown reason I was being punished. I promised myself that I would be more vigilant in the future. I would make sure I always said my prayers. Maybe then, I wouldn't have the dream of being in hell with the devil. Maybe then, HE wouldn't come in and hurt me.*

*Sometime later, I finally drifted off to sleep, pondering the difference between real life and nightmares. Which was worse? Which was more real? I eventually acknowledged that my worst nightmares occurred not when I was asleep, but when I awoke.*

*My greatest fears, of course, centered on the next visit—when would it be? I have no recollection how many times these nocturnal visits occurred; only that I knew I would be stained forever because of them ... stained forever like ink on a brand new white shirt I might wear to church.*

\* \* \* \* \* \*

When this memory returned, much later in my life ... I have to admit it broke my heart. How could anyone, much less a father, wreak such degradation and destruction on a child ... on me?

*Every 98 seconds an American is*
*sexually assaulted.*

—RAINN (Rape, Abuse & Incest National Network),
NCSV (National Crime Victimization Survey),
Dept. of Justice's Bureau of Justice Statistics

.

## CHAPTER 1

# HOW THIS BOOK'S TITLE CAME TO BE

It was a dream that provided the title to this book—a dream that was pulled from an actual event in my past.

The event took place when I was fifteen years old. The situation that created it began when my sister married a man at an early age—perhaps as her own way of escaping our father's insanity.

Her new husband's stepfather, a B-movie producer from Hollywood, owned a dude ranch in the tiny town of Pinedale, Wyoming, about an hour and a half south of Jackson Hole, Wyoming. The father-in-law invited me to work at the ranch for the summer. This absolutely gorgeous setting proved to be a slice of heaven for me. I went horse-back riding and fishing, attended rodeos and cattle drives followed by their roundup, roping and branding. I witnessed many wild animal sightings and enjoyed square dances and singing around the campfire. It all seemed part of a dream come true for a month or so.

The ambience radically changed, however, when my father showed up. A situation had arisen in the Pinedale area when a grizzly bear began killing cattle and game. One of the local ranchers informed us he had found a downed deer that had been partially eaten and saw evidence left by the bear that it had tried to camouflage the carcass so it could return later to finish it.

My father, probably trying to appear as "the great hunter," had volunteered himself and proposed the idea of locating the hiding spot, waiting for the bear to return, and then killing it. As the instigator, naturally my father made himself the "leader," followed by me, with the ranch hand/cowboy named Riley bringing up the rear on this safari hunt.

Trekking up the steep mountain at an already high elevation of 9,000 feet, I was blind-sided by my father suddenly whipping around to hiss at me in a most vile manner, "Shut up, goddamn it. You're breathing too loud!"

Any excitement I had felt at our adventure was vanquished as I was immediately embarrassed and ashamed. These two themes played prominent roles in my life growing up in the Carwile family. I felt even worse this time because the cowboy who had followed closely behind me was a man I respected and wanted to impress. Fifteen years old and as insecure as most teenagers, I turned to look at Riley only to observe his own red face from embarrassment. All he could do was shake his head in discomfort before looking down at the ground. It seemed that degradation of one human by another engenders humiliation on all present.

Move ahead forty years to when I was awakened by my wife, next to me in our bed, as she tried to wrest me from my dream. With urgency, she shook me. "Ernie, wake up! You're crying in your sleep."

After sitting up, she gently prodded, "Wow. You've never done that before. Why were you crying? What were you dreaming?"

Wiping the tears from my eyes, I related the

incident of hunting the bear.

Gently she said, "Ernie, I realize that was an embarrassing thing for your father to say to you ... but ... that story was mild compared to so many of the other stories you've shared with me."

Shaking my head in disagreement, I lay back down. Even in a half-state of awareness, I was distraught and pleaded with her, "Oh Mary, it was so sad ... *Why, even the trees were crying.*"

Pausing only briefly, she abruptly shook me awake again exclaiming, "Ernie, that's the title you've been searching for. Don't you see? That's the title of your book— 'EVEN THE TREES WERE CRYING!'"

The following morning, my wife and I reflected upon why we felt so strongly about this title. After much discussion, we concluded that it represented something universal, something so insightful that it ignited recognition, like maybe a secret code that would attract the people who needed to read it. *In fact, if you are reading this book, perhaps there is a reason for your selecting it.*

These insights were followed by a deeper understanding that, perhaps, the *crying trees* represented the abysmal sadness only those who have been raped and sexually abused feel in their core self; a grievous bleakness we feel that others can't understand nor comprehend.

Though my wife had a pretty much fairy tale kind of life growing up in South Dakota and had no firsthand understanding of what I had experienced, she sensed the power in the title's words. For me, the image of the weeping trees symbolized a conglomeration of my painful memories; it portrayed my prolific sadness and confusion. How could one individual treat another so horrifically, much less a father to a son?

*EVEN THE TREES WERE CRYING* will not flinch from the specifics of what sexual abuse entails. It will unveil the debilitating effects of such abuse, delineate signs to look for in loved ones, and, most importantly, reveal the secrets to healing from this ugly perversity that secretly plagues humankind.

\* \* \* \* \* \*

Let me share some crucially important facts. While there is some disagreement in the numbers as they increase each year as more victims step forward, here are some current estimates from a study done by Finkelhor, D., Hotaling, G., Lewis, I.A., & Smith (1990):

> One out of every 4 females is sexually abused;
> One out of every 6 males is sexually abused.

This means that approximately 20% of the U.S. population of 300 million, or SIXTY MILLION Americans, are living their lives and trying to function normally while being severely damaged. This number, for perspective, I believe is more than the total number of people who died from wars, cancer or other diseases and all the traffic fatalities in the United States. Try to imagine the corrosive anger, potential violence and other destructive behaviors these tens of millions of Americans carry with them.

Furthermore, consider these questions: What percentage of violent crimes of assault, rape, and murder were, and are, perpetrated by those influenced by sexual abuse (SA) ... 50%, 60%, or 80%? How many angry, seething, abused men and women are then perpetuating this cycle of abuse onto themselves, their children, and others? And, could SA be the worst of the "sins of the fathers" (Exodus 20:5) the Bible refers to?

*We have seen the enemy ... and the enemy is us!*

—POGO
Newspaper Cartoon

*75% of rape victims require medical care*
*after the attack.*

—Bureau of Justice Statistics, 1994

## Chapter 2

## Background Information

Life is an *inside job*, meaning that what happens on the *outside* doesn't matter as much as how we react to it, how we perceive every event from the *inside*.

In an attempt to describe this experience we call *life*, someone thought up the adage or metaphor that may best describe it: "Life is like a poker game; it's not the cards you are dealt that count, but how you *play* the ones you get."

Certainly, some of us are given worse cards than others, but the same wisdom applies: *how we play the ones we are given,* or who knows, maybe we are the ones who actually choose those specific adversities/

cards we experience—this is what counts.

Sexual abuse, sometimes referred to as "the soul killer," may be one of the worst struggles a human being may have to face because of its powerful and destructive effects upon the victims. There is even proof that it alters the brain's cell structure and may change one's genetic/DNA make-up.

If you missed the above shocking point, let me restate it: *childhood sexual abuse can alter the victim's DNA.* "A Voice for the Innocent" organization learned that scientists and researchers have discovered, for the first time, that childhood trauma leaves a mark on the DNA of some victims, specifically in three genes: the FKBP5, the 5-HTTLPR and the CRHR1.

Most of us think that DNA is like a pattern, or a mold, but it is not. Just as one director of a play will direct it according to his/her preferences or creative ideas, another director will direct it differently. Both are using the same script though each plays it out differently.

I don't want to bog this down with the technicalities of just how the DNA change occurs as well as the negative effects it has upon the body and neural functioning, but the overwhelming concern is that SA is much more than just the physical and emotional degradation that takes place, for its severity extends to the core of who we are—our DNA. Perhaps, when this discovery is finally received by our world, it just might provide the greatest impetus for eradicating all abuse.

\* \* \* \* \* \*

While we cannot go back and erase the past, the only possible solution is to learn how to play the cards we were dealt in a different fashion than the way we've perhaps been trying to deal with it, i.e. denial, dissociation, abusing alcohol and other drugs, extreme anger or complete stoicism, promiscuity, abhorrence towards sex, depression, cutting oneself, bulimia, or withdrawal along with a plethora of other destructive behaviors.

Fortunately, relatively new healing techniques have arisen from the ashes. Unfortunately, there are few agreements among therapists as to which are the most effective. The purpose of this book is to share the healing techniques **that worked for me**, and, perhaps, might work for you. Keep in mind what works for one individual may not work for another. The vital step is to keep looking until the right connection is made.

* * * * * *

One of the most powerful poems I have come across is attributed to an anonymous Confederate soldier.

> I asked God for strength,
> that I might achieve,
> I was made weak, that I might
> learn to humbly obey.
>
> I asked for health, that I might
> do greater things,
> I was given infirmity that I might
> do better things.
>
> I asked for riches, that I might
> be happy,
> I was given poverty that I might
> be wise.
>
> I asked for power, that I might
> have the praise of men,

I was given weakness that I might
feel the need of God.

I asked for all things, that I might
enjoy life,
I was given life that I might
enjoy all things.

I got nothing that I asked for—
but everything I had [secretly] hoped for.

Almost despite myself, my
unspoken prayers were answered.

I am among all men,
most richly blessed.

I remember the first time I read the powerful and contagious words from the poem, "I got nothing that I asked for—but everything I had [secretly] hoped for." Somehow, this writing and those particular lines awoke some latent, sleeping memory in me that had been lying-in-wait to be awakened, and its remembrance returned feelings that had reverberated through my soul for decades. These feelings and thoughts then ignited a bizarre new idea: *What if the worst events in my life, the most significant and seemingly destructive occurrences that took place and left me emotionally and physically crippled, eventually proved to not be the worst things but were the necessary and needed lessons vital to achieving the real purpose of my life's journey?*

\* \* \* \* \* \*

*Again, 20% of the 300,000,000 Americans, or 60,000,000 humans—one in every five people you see every day—have been sexually assaulted and, perhaps, continue to be sexually abused.*

*Have you been sexually abused? Do you know or suspect anyone who has been?*

\* \* \* \* \* \*

**Pedophile.** What do you do if a family member is a pedophile? How does it affect you when that person is your *father or mother, uncle or grandfather?* How do you cope when their horrific actions were perpetrated on you as a little boy or girl? As a teenager? As an adult? How do you live when every aspect of your life has been jaded and tainted by these unspeakable deeds? How did—how could—God allow such a thing to occur? Like the quote at the beginning of the book said, **"God must be very wise and strong to give humans the free will to commit their atrocities on one another ... I could never be God; I mean, I would never give them *that* much freedom."**

I am a sixty-nine-year old male who, for the first thirty years of my life, had no memories of the sexual abuse committed by my father. I always sensed something was wrong with me—strange dreams, depression, unhappiness, and an inability to enjoy good grades or a successful performance in sports or theater or art, beleaguered by feelings of inadequacy—but had no idea as to the source of this insight. Amnesia may seem hard to believe/understand, but it has been recorded that nearly one-half of the sexually abused had no memories until *awakened* at some point. If this had not happened to me, I would certainly agree with those who have trouble comprehending this phenomenon—who doubt the non-remembrance claim.

After the first memories began surfacing when I was in my thirties, I spent the next thirty-eight years struggling to heal. Not until the last sixteen of those years did I stumble upon new healing methods and ideas that led to *actual healing*, something I was beginning to believe would never happen. Believe me when I say that I could not share this journey, my insights, or these real healing methods unless I had been down in the trenches with every one of you who are going through this. All of us, who have been sexually abused, regardless of how severely, are members of a club no one wants to join. We are the only ones who speak this language and the only ones who can truly understand the pain, confusion, and oddity each one of us feels.

*This is the crux of this book:* I discovered how to heal and ***let me assure you that you can, too,*** just as sure as God made little green apples.

* * * * * *

On the outside, I looked normal; no, actually better than normal. Here is my external biography:

*I was born in Munich, Germany, and lived throughout the world. Graduating from the University of Missouri, I later attended graduate school at Iliff School of Theology in Denver, Colorado.*

*My father was an Air Force Officer, navigator for USAF Chief of Staff General Curtis Lemay. We moved frequently, and I attended, I think, fourteen different schools growing up.*

*I had sisters who were identical twins and, on the outside, we looked like the perfect military family, and were frequently complimented for this very appearance. My mother was a stay-at-home mom and a great cook.*

*After high school, I sold cemetery plots door-to-door in Hannibal, Missouri, believe it or not, and, while attending college, I drove huge trucks for Peabody Coal Mine. Some of my other careers included being an Air Force officer, heavyweight boxer, real estate developer, and a Methodist and Congregational minister.*

Again, this is how I looked from the *outside*. *Inside*, I sensed something was off, that a germ resided in me that had been spreading its destructive tentacles, often leaving me to desperately try to survive the horrid thoughts, feelings, and dreams that filled my daily inner life. I pedaled hard, trying to keep ahead of some dark, evil force. Most likely, you would never have known anything was amiss, were you to view me from the outside. I projected myself as someone confident and healthy, all the while hiding behind whatever mask I deemed necessary for the time.

* * * * * *

*One most intriguing insight arose while writing this book, something so unexpected— something completely unforeseen. An idea emerged that may perplex you as it continues haunting me. I'll identify this insight in later chapters.*

*Males are the abusers 80-95% of cases.*

—Thoringer, D., et al., 1988

## CHAPTER 3

# COPING MECHANISMS

Because I had been unable to remember the sexual abuse (SA) until the age of around thirty, it is difficult to know the exact age it began. My *guesstimate*, reinforced by feelings and dream-like memories, is that my sexual abuse started around the age of five when we lived in Plattsmouth, Nebraska. **How did I block out those memories** for the twenty-plus prior years?

## DISSOCIATION

The first coping skill I utilized sprang up *unconsciously*; I had no awareness that I was using it. *Dissociation* is a tactic our phenomenal minds incorporate when the shock of something is simply too great to grasp. It allows the conscious mind to *disappear*—to remove itself from the present, horrible situation and go somewhere else. I never figured out where my consciousness went during my dissociative events.

In my early thirties, I entered seminary/graduate school, probably as a desperate, unconscious attempt at seeking another way to heal through religion. During my third year there, I was contacted by my parents and informed of my favorite grandfather's death in Texas. I immediately flew there and stayed at a motel that my father had arranged for the family members. That day, while talking to my parents in their room, my mother suddenly said she had to leave the room for something. It was then, when we were alone, my father abruptly began, inexplicably, to talk about his penis implant, the surgery that took place after his prostrate was removed while he was treated for cancer. Apparently, this implant allowed him to continue to perform sexually.

I remember him next asking if I wanted to see it.

Responding "No" didn't stop him. He began making a very familiar, strange, sucking noise with his lips and teeth, a sound I remembered from my most fearsome childhood memories. He then became more animatedly aggressive, unzipped his pants, and boldly directed me to "Look at this" while walking towards me, holding his penis.

Looking back now, I realize that this was the first time I remembered the early stages of my dissociation process that I went through—that I had been going through most of my life:

*I suddenly became conscious of the loud sound/noise of wind blowing in my ears followed by my awareness that the blinking of my eyes had slowed down to such a degree it seemed each blink took seconds to complete its process, not the normal instantaneous "blink of an eye." Then, somehow, my consciousness floated away to some other place.*

My next awareness in the motel room was hearing a knocking at the room's door followed by my father quickly putting his penis back in his pants as he hurried to let my mother back in the room; I have no further memories after that; everything seemed to be in a fog.

Later, I was able to connect this dissociation remembrance with the first SA memory of my father coming into my room at night. When I was fifteen, we were living in the Commanders' Quarters at Mather A.F.B. in Sacramento, California. I remembered awakening and looking down to see that my bedcovers had been pulled down, along with my underwear and my father doing something with my genitals while shining a light on them. I remembered then that this was when the dissociation kicked in: the wind blowing noisily in my ears and my eyelids blinking preposterously slow. I think I might have said, "No!" but my consciousness evaporated along with all further memories.

Much later, I remembered researching this seemingly frightening term—dissociation or *Dissociative Disorder* as it is more formally termed. I read: "a person experiencing such a traumatic event will pull away from the present time and situation; they will feel detached, as if floating, or in another world; simply put, when the emotional pain or emotional memory is more than a person can cope with, they dissociate or escape from the pain; it is the mind's way of coping from an intolerable life experience; it is a detachment from reality."

Floored by my discovery because it was exactly what I had been experiencing, I recalled feeling how bizarre it was to read about some weird psychological disorder that I myself had lived through and was now remembering/discovering; one that I had no awareness of before.

Reading further, I found an array of psychologists and psychiatrists who emphasized the power of the mind in possessing such a protective mechanism. I also read a negative article in the magazine, *Psychology Today*. There was an article proclaiming "Dissociation is not a life skill." Despite this assertion, I can personally attest it was a phenomenal life skill I used when overwhelmed with events that defied rational thinking.

Of note is the question I have sought to answer: Where did my consciousness go when I left the scene? Unfortunately, no answer has been found and I still frequently wonder about it.

\* \* \* \* \* \*

## DRUGS

The second most powerful and vital coping mechanism that allowed me to continue with life was drugs. This sounds contrary to rational thinking and, perhaps, even ridiculous, but one can only incorporate what one knows, tries, and discovers that works. Drugs kept me alive and, without them, I may have ended my life at some point earlier.

Fortunately, or unfortunately, with all drug usage, you eventually have to *pay the piper* as I surely did.

I began sampling alcohol at the age of ten after we moved to the island of Guam and continued through high school where my drinking accelerated to almost every weekend. With college came more alcohol—more frequently and in greater volume. Eventually, because of a recurring ulcer, I was forced to admit I had a serious problem with alcohol; I stopped drinking for two years during my first marriage.

All addictions are deceitful; they start off so innocently while foreshadowing a dependency.

At the age of thirty, after my first marriage

ended, drinking again became a problem. Entering seminary, I knew I had to do something to stop my alcohol consumption. Having some deep-seated understanding that I needed something to provide a break from the bleak dark feelings, memories, and dreams, I switched to marijuana, "using" most every night and all day long on my days off while a minister. Interestingly, the twelve or so years I smoked grass, I had little desire for alcohol. Good, right? Nope, for the underlying cause or source of my need to escape persisted.

After smoking for a quite a period, I realized this crutch had become a full-fledged addiction, one I was unable to stop at will. And I must mention that I had added the drug speed to go along with my pot smoking. The speed provided not only a better high but, also, decreased my sweets consumption and eating everything in the refrigerator. Additionally, to offset my prodigious appetite from smoking weed, I had been forcing my finger down my throat to vomit up the huge amounts of food I had been consuming—I was bulimic.

These drugs did decrease my physical pain from an earlier spinal injury while boxing in the Air Force and my emotional pain from the SA. Without any doubt in my mind and body, these drugs allowed me to keep hanging on. They enabled me to be highly functional during the daytime as long as I could escape in the evenings.

We have all heard that using one drug often leads to using others. This proved true for me as well. As my physical and emotional pain continued increasing, I incorporated even more detrimental drugs into my routine. Whereas my past drugs of choice had been alcohol, marijuana, and speed, I now upped the ante.

For my physical pain, legal, doctor-prescribed Percocets became an intimate part of my daily life. With their multiplying effects when combined with alcohol, they, at first, proved to be a godsend. As for the emotional pain, it too benefited greatly. In my youth, I had always presumed the internal issues I secretly felt would go away with adulthood, but of course, becoming an adult proved this to be false. What actually happened was that these emotional problems intensified. I sensed—knew—that I was in deep doo-doo, for my well-being was in a faster downhill slide now than ever before.

My solution? The only solution I knew that would temporarily work was new and more destructive drugs; thus, cocaine and crack entered the picture. I remember the first time I regularly started using cocaine. After randomly sampling it five or six times, I finally purchased a large quantity still partially in the form of a block, which one then had to chop up to snort. I remembered thinking, if I did this, I would be totally giving up on life. With little hesitation, I lowered my whole face and nose into the pile of freshly razor-chopped white powder and snorted a huge amount. The effect: instantaneous change from the dark grim feelings and thoughts to a pleasant glow, though edgier and faster-paced than the effect from Percocets, speed, alcohol, and marijuana.

Cocaine proved to be a truly evil drug. Like the others, it crept into my daily routine like the life-saving pussycat I hoped it might be. Two snorts and my foreboding blackness vanished into nothingness. Each new daily routine began with cereal and ice-cold milk loaded with sugar in the morning. Then, around 10:30 a.m., I would chew two Percocets to diminish my growing physical pain. I chewed them forty-five minutes before eating or drinking to give the Percocet time to kick in and amplify the effects from consuming a couple of gin martinis.

Following lunch (the only real sustenance I would eat each day), I would return to the car and take my first cocaine snorts of the day, then drive home to supplement my body with marijuana and more cocaine for the remainder of the day and far into the night. To finally stop each day and sleep, I discovered I needed illegal prescriptions of Xanax. After swallowing three or so, sleep came easily. Upon awakening in the morning, the cycle was repeated.

The cocaine addiction lasted eighteen long months, the last twelve of them pure hell. My weight plummeted; my nose and sinuses were constantly stopped up. Soon, the nose bleeds began, and getting to sleep at night became a major issue. I initially believed that, with each drug usage, I was exhibiting freedom to choose my lifestyle: to use or not to use. I ended up, like all addicts do, not with freedom but with a self-made prison.

Miraculously (I can't explain how I did it), I broke this near-fatal addiction with cocaine cold turkey though I continued with the Percocets for the physical pain and alcohol to numb my mind. But I was soon, again, at the end of my rope—still in great physical pain, great emotional torment, and deeper depression with serious suicidal thoughts.

"Hell is not a place you go to; it is a state of mind."

My mind slowly tried to heal itself and eventually cycled back to possessing some bit of clarity. Once again I knew I had to find some healing from this hell I found myself in. As far as the Percocets, I had a small epiphany, which produced the realization that, to stop using, all I had to do was discard my back cache of the drug and cancel my monthly prescription ... which I did. I soon discovered I had not been as addicted to them as I had with the other drugs, probably because I had pretty much limited myself to the 2-4 pills a day as prescribed by a doctor. As for the continuing physical pain, I had no solution other than dabbling with physical exercises.

My next epiphany disclosed that I somehow had the amazing ability to simply quit—almost instantly and with less drama than many other people experience—most of the drugs I had been imbibing in:

gone were the cocaine, speed, crack, Percocets, and marijuana. However, the last remaining drug—alcohol—proved *the* most difficult to stop.

Nothing I tried worked: drinking only beer and wine—no hard stuff; limiting the number of drinks I had; not drinking alone; never drinking in the morning; drinking only at home; never having it in the house; never drinking before 5 o'clock; drinking only at parties; switching from gin to vodka (which I hated); drinking only *natural* wines; moving to a new area; more physical exercise; reading inspirational books; seeing a therapist; going to health farms/rehabs; and yada, yada, yada. I found no lasting results. Nothing worked, leaving me disheartened after every failure. This all left me with one last dreaded possibility, the one to which I had always sworn I would never succumb (deathmarch drumbeats): AA meetings.

I know you have probably mentally and verbally rebuffed every argument for the need to try AA. I know. I did, too. But, guess what? It eventually worked and proved the only way I could stop drinking!

My first meeting found me criticizing every one

of their procedures—the twelve steps and philosophy—as sheer bullshit. That is, until I continued to attend and everything slowly changed. Only after wearing down all my defenses did the Twelve-Step Program begin to make sense, and I started perceiving the meetings as the greatest source of free counseling for everyday life issues for anybody, not only for alcoholics.

However, this was *not* the end of my alcohol addiction. Now able to stop all drug usage and alcohol drinking, at least part of the time, I had eliminated my ability to access physical and emotional relief through them; thus, releasing the dark memories, dreams, and blocked thoughts. As clearer remembrances of the abuses and my detrimental solutions ran wild during the time periods when I did not drink, I soon discovered the most destructive thought that had always been present.

## SUICIDAL THOUGHTS

Though only slightly aware that it lurked in my shadow, I became conscious of just how pervasively my *suicidal thinking* had been ingrained throughout my life. The psychological, physical, and sexual abuses I had experienced from my father had made the idea of suicide an appealing option. Unaware that most people did not consider suicide, I simply thought this was normal. Now, for perhaps the first time in my life, I became acutely aware of just how horrid my life had been. The drugs were no longer a daily respite from the internal darkness.

With this new understanding and with rational intent, while dog-tired over just trying to survive, on July 28, 2011, **I committed suicide.**

I had begun to rationally contemplate it over the previous six months; had even discussed it with a men's group to which I belonged, but, perhaps like the other members, never thought I would really carry it out. Until one night, with forethought and purpose, I swallowed ten oxycontin, twenty Percocets, and fifty to sixty (a large handful) of atenolol along with a fifth of gin. Crawling into bed, I was content to leave this miserable life I had been given.

Upon awakening the next morning, I was shocked (and disappointed) to still be here.

Confused at first, and consciously knowing that

my death should have taken place after my massive intake of drugs and alcohol, a new revelation occurred. Maybe I had not died for some reason, some purpose, and it was, simply, not my time to die. I immediately called the therapist with whom I had, ironically, made an appointment with that very day and told her openly what I had done. With no hesitation, she told me to hang up and go to a hospital where I could be put in a 72-hour lockdown; which I did. I had a friend drive me to the hospital.

If you've never been to a psych ward, the experience is a real eye-opener. A good example is what I discovered upon opening my bedroom door the first morning. My introductory interaction with another patient came when I was approached by a man walking slowly up and down the corridor, a Bible in each hand loudly espousing Biblical damnations for our world.

A bit stunned over its weirdness, I edged past him and searched for the kitchen and breakfast. After selecting my choices, I sat at a table with others. What most surprised me was that, while many at the table had recently attempted suicide, an outside observer would never have known from the facial expressions, conversations, and overall milieu at the table. I kept thinking to myself *how odd that no one even mentions what they were in for but carries on as if nothing has happened. I also questioned myself as to how in the hell was I going to last in here for the next seventy-two hours.*

Well, I did make it through and, seventy-two hours later, I exited the hospital and went immediately to an AA meeting where I shared what I had done.

For some unexplainable reason, over the next six months, I was able to completely stop all alcohol … that is, until I was notified that my father had died on my *birthday, November 15th*. This caused my anger to explode; mostly for regretting never physically harming him for doing what he had done to me, perhaps even torturing or killing him. Bursting inside and unable to deal with the rage I was feeling, I resorted to my only known method of dealing with my extreme emotions—I got drunk! Fortunately, as it turned out, it was only for that one night. The next morning, I checked out of the hotel in the Denver Tech Center where I had holed myself up for my binge and have never had another drink of alcohol.

Before this event, I believed—as many other people do—that the act of suicide is basically a "selfish" action. After making the decision to do it and diligently trying to accomplish it, I now acutely understand selfishness has *nothing to do with it.* I now know that, when the perceived pain someone is feeling is simply too great and all hope has vanished in the wind, suicide is a most viable option. And only someone who has been there can comprehend this.

I have also come to some other conclusions about my suicide attempt.

First, even though I was not successful in killing myself, my decision to do so was not a plea for help, nor a confused, irrational choice I made without forethought. It was, in fact, an explicit and categorically decisive action taken to remove myself from my internally, intolerable life.

That said and affirmed, I later came to understand my suicide attempt was the action that, ironically, saved my life! You see, looking back, I eventually recognized, for whatever reason, this was the event that initiated the *withdrawal of the darkness that had encompassed my life. Following this dire choice, somehow, all the blackness, repressed memories, and detestable dreams began vanishing into the ether.* I was left with a sense of normalcy I had never experienced before. Why or how this happened, I have no rational explanation.

**Please do not misunderstand my purpose in sharing this part of my story as an excuse for you, too, to attempt suicide.** Suicide is a permanent solution to a temporary problem, and, if you choose it, you may not have the opportunity to overcome the adversities that have been presented in your life. I have no answer as to why my circumstances worked out the way it did; all I know is that this is my journey.

*I fervently urge you to contact a hospital if you become suicidal, or simply call 911. You may not believe this right now, but the world needs you for there is and never will be another person like you in all of eternity.*

*Like rape, child molestation is an underreported crime; only 1-10% is ever disclosed.*

—FBI Law Enforcement Bulletin

## CHAPTER 4

# THE SIGNS OF SEXUAL ABUSE

**B**efore we proceed further, it is important for you, the reader, to be aware of the **signs of sexual abuse**. Why? So you can recognize them in your loved ones, students, and employees.

\* \* \* \* \* \*

Despite our society's vigorous attempts to deny the existence of SA, there are many obvious signs present in children, teens, and adults. Whether you are a person seeking to discover the source of your own misery, or you are a parent, teacher, or grandparent desiring to know what to look for in your loved ones or students, there are often obvious warning indications. You may have to overcome the blindness of denial to recognize what may be before your very eyes.

For me, before the memories returned, a menu of visible indications was present from an early age:

- Medicating with alcohol and cigarettes by the age of ten;

- Vague awareness of the Obsessive-Compulsive-Disorder (OCD) of counting the number of steps and letters in words;

- Looking for odd or even numbers on signs and other writings—this began at an early age and continues to this day;

- Early stuttering (obviously, not all stuttering comes from abuse);

- Regularly recurring horrible, sinister dreams when I would wake up screaming in the night, drenched in sweat. (One bizarre dream I had multiple times involved waking up at night, knowing something was wrong, going down-stairs to discover my mother and twin sisters lying inert on the floor. The smell of feces was strong and, when I approached them, I saw their physical bodies had been replaced with feces in their exact forms with arms, legs, and the same facial shapes).

- Fighting with other boys beginning around the age of six or seven and continuing into my early twenties, including joining the Air Force Boxing Team (deep-seated anger was always present).

Along with contracting nearly every childhood disease, I had recurring serious episodes with coughing and respiratory problems three to four times every year. (I later came to understand that getting sick kept me safe from my father's nightly attentions). I developed ulcers by the age of ten.

Much later in life, when I was in the process of participating in Eye Movement Desensitization and Reprocessing (EMDR), a psychological technique you'll read more about later in the book, I focused with ferocity on dredging up the past memories and the feelings they evoked, surrounding my whole realm of SA. For some inexplicable reason, during this intense time, I realized I had acquired the uncanny ability to identify others who had been sexually abused. I could be in a room filled with many people or involved in a one-to-one interaction. In one instant, I could tell. Does this seem impossible? It's like a black friend of mine, who told me he could "walk into a room and pick out the racists.'" There are signs openly present, but, unless you've been there yourself or are aware, your blindness and your prejudices keep you from seeing.

Only after I had accumulated a long list of characteristics a sexually abused person may exhibit was I able to understand how I could read an abused person's signals.

Here is a rather extensive list of most of the characteristics that the abused carry with them:

> Gradual or sudden changes in behavior (withdrawn, fearful, depressed);

> Sudden exhibition of aggressive/disruptive behavior;

> Cruelty to pets;

> Recurring nightmares;

> Sudden change, displaying immature

behavior;

➢ Expressing affection in inappropriate ways for someone their age;

➢ Inappropriately exposing their body/genital parts at home or in public;

➢ Acting out inappropriate sexual play;

➢ Excessive masturbation;

➢ Premature maturity seen in acting or dressing older/suggestively;

➢ Wearing many layers of clothing;

➢ Pretending to be sick or actually becoming sick frequently;

➢ Loss or lack of interest in school, friends, sports, etc.;

➢ Bed wetting, soiling and playing with feces;

➢ Excessive bathing;

➢ Sexual inferences in school work;

➢ Overly compulsive behavior;

➢ Early substance abuse;

➢ Fears and phobias;

➢ Running away;

➢ Sleep problems;

➢ Fire starting.

Especially for Pre-teens and Teenagers:

➢ Extreme and/or unexplained anger;

➢ Running away;

➢ Delinquent behavior;

➢ Low self-esteem;

➢ Self-Destructive behavior/self-harming, e.g., cutting, self-mutilation, and burning oneself;

➢ Seductive and promiscuous behavior;

➢ Addictions;

➢ Sudden change in school work and behaviors;

➢ Eating disorders;

➤ Greater anxiety;

➤ Suicidal thoughts.

After discovering these characteristics, I knew I could have been a poster boy for SA. Obviously, not all children or teens or adults showing these signs have been sexually abused, but if the signs are picked up, it may be worth further investigation. One stronger indication that sexual abuse has occurred arises from claims made by victims themselves. For males, when one has made an abuse claim, *only 1% of such claims have been disproved. With females,* the percentage is slightly higher because of the rare tendency when it was found to have been initiated by an angry mother wishing to degrade her husband, or a female wishing to harm a male with this extreme and detrimental claim. However, regardless of the sex, when a claim is made it must be considered.

\* \* \* \* \* \*

For me, promiscuity came early. We now understand that, after sexual abuse, the victim either becomes obsessive about sex or wants nothing to do with it. I began exploring sex with females on the island of Guam at the age of eleven and discovered masturbation at age twelve. I know that every young man *believes they alone* masturbate too frequently, which is where such myths as going blind or developing hairy palms originated, but mine was truly off the wall. Later in life, while in a session with a female therapist who inquired how often I masturbated, I thought first before replying, "Fifteen to twenty times."

"A month?" she asked with eyebrows arched.

"No," I sheepishly admitted, "a week." I can still remember her attempts at masking her initial reaction. Promiscuity remained an integral part of my life because it was the only time I could achieve intimacy.

I had no concept of boundaries. I remember visiting a friend and opening a closed bathroom door only to find my friend's angry sister sitting on the toilet, berating me for opening the closed door to a bathroom. Truly embarrassed over what I had done, I had no sense of my inappropriateness; a closed door meant nothing to my father and, therefore, to the rest of the family; only a locked door meant something—was honored.

Another bizarre example of lack of bound-aries, privacy, or learned inappropriate behavior in my home life, but one I didn't know was peculiar behavior, often occurred when my father returned from a flying assignment. As a navigator for the Chief of Staff of the Air Force, he often flew all over the world. Upon his return home, my father would gather my mother, twin sisters, and me into the bathroom while he had a bowel movement. I vividly recall the horrible stench, the veins in his neck enlarging as he strained to relieve himself, and the sounds of feces dropping into the toilet. Yes, I did have an inkling this was quite inappropriate behavior for our culture, but I overrode my doubting with the family's apparent belief that it was normal.

From age ten to twenty, I suffered at least one major accident every year: a severely burnt face and neck, a disease that caused painful swelling in both knees, ulcers, a broken big toe, a shattered left kneecap, dislocated right kneecap, broken thumb, and crushed vertebrae. (Later, I would finally come to understand that these "accidents" were my first, unconscious attempts at killing myself.) On one hand, you might have thought I was just an accident-prone kid; or, somebody—a coach, teacher, neighbor, relative—might have looked a little deeper to find the real source of these regularly occurring accidents or, at least, asked questions.

I remember reading Scott Peck's book, *The Road Less Traveled,* and especially the first line, "Life is difficult." My follow-up thought to this profound statement was "No shit, Sherlock!"

Only after researching everything about the destructive act of sexual abuse did I realize just how pervasive it was despite society's and our world's attempts to deny it; to wear blinders as to its existence.

*"The world breaks everyone, and afterward, many are strong in the broken places."*

—Ernest Hemingway, *A Farewell to Arms*

*"Interestingly, the serial killer has the same personality characteristics as sex offenders against children."*

—Dr. Mace Knapp,
Nevada State Prison Psychologist

## CHAPTER 5

# GROOMING

*Grooming* is the term used to describe how a sexual abuser manipulates a victim and their family into allowing a child to be abused. The common techniques can be exceptionally subtle and are often highly effective. Here is a real-life story of a grooming process from a lady who was kind enough to share her story here.

*I was a single, divorced mother of two boys: ages one and seven, living in a small mountain town in Colorado in the 1980's. Word around town was that a new Scout Master had just moved to town and was starting a Cub Scout troop. My own dad had been very active in scouting so I was one of the first to sign up my oldest son. The Scout Master, I learned his name was Denny, was a single man with a son of his own, about the same age as my son. He seemed nice enough when we met; eager to get to know the boys and their parents. He was always friendly when I'd see him in our small town and soon he invited me to lunch; nothing but a cordial way to get to know each other, nothing more. We talked of scouting and of our boys. He mentioned he'd love to take his son to Disney World and then added if I'd like he would even take my son along. I was thrilled at the idea since I knew I'd never be able to afford a trip like that for my boys. We talked about the Boy Scout Jamboree that was scheduled in a nearby town in a couple of weeks and I shared that I'd planned to be leaving on vacation a few days after the Jamboree. I also told him I didn't yet have a sitter for my oldest son while I was away.*

*A few days later he called with a tempting*

*offer for me. He said my son could spend the night with him and his son the night before Jamboree since the bus was leaving from the school so very early in the morning. "That way you don't have to get the baby up and dressed so early to get your son to the bus." Wow. What a relief that was. That was to be on a Friday night; the Jamboree was Saturday and Sunday. He also suggested that it would be great for "the baby" and I to join him and the boys (mine and his) for dinner on Sunday after they'd returned from the Jamboree. Again, thrilled, I'd accepted his offer. He was a caterer and a great cook, I'd heard around town. By the way, this was never about him pursuing me for a possible relationship. Never.*

*He had also offered to let my son stay at their condo while I went on my first-ever ocean vacation. As it turned out, my son was to have stayed the night before the Jamboree, and the next 3 nights before I left for vacation in a week. "No sense packing him up and going back and forth. This gives you time ...."*

*Of course I never saw it in the moment, but his plan gave him time, as well.*

*The baby and I went to his door on that Sunday evening for dinner. The door was a bit ajar and when I knocked, the door opened. In front of me, across the room, my son was sitting on Denny's lap. I was alarmed. Something inside me shifted, but then there were hugs, giggles, dinner, hugs again, and I went home with the baby. Something inside me was not quite settled but I didn't know what it was.*

*Monday morning, my son called me to see if I'd bring him some of his toy trucks. And then he added, "Oh, and mom?" "What?" I asked him. After a too long pause, he added, "Oh ... nothing." But I knew. I just knew something was "off."*

*I drove the few miles to Denny's condo in minutes to find my son and Denny's son playing outside in the dirt. His son was peculiar, I'd noticed, and hadn't said but a few words any time I'd ever seen him, including at dinner the night before. I opened my car door to chat with my son and give him his toys. He wasn't acting like himself. He was quiet and kept kicking at the dirt under his feet. I inquired a bit and then finally just asked him if he needed to tell me something. I was gentle. He and I were very close and I knew he felt safe to talk to me. He didn't give up his reason for a while but, after reminding him I was going on vacation and I wouldn't see him for a week or so, he talked. "Denny's been touching me," he started. "Where?!" was my first response. I will never forget the look on that precious face as he jerked his head and looked directly in my eyes. "You know where!" he firmly said.*

*Oh yes, I knew where. I grabbed my son and put him in the car, leaving the other boy alone in my haste and panic. Of course, he said nothing in protest or wonder. Did he know, too? Was he really Denny's son?*

*I stopped at the office at the condo where Denny was working as the property manager and said just one thing. "I'm taking my son."*

*His reply? "Oh, I didn't know the boys were fighting."*

*I'd said nothing of the sort. I just left and drove home, shaking all over. I went back alone to Denny's apartment that evening and knocked again on the partially open door and was told to come in. I walked in, said only, "I'm here to get my son's things."*

*Again ... "I didn't know the boys were fighting" was his reply. I hadn't said that, ever. His son sat on the floor blankly staring at the TV. Not a word was said; not a typical reaction from a boy who was having a sleepover for a week. No whining, "Where's your son?" or "Dad, why isn't [Ross] coming back?" Nothing. What did he know? What had he experienced? Denny was gone when I returned from vacation. I never found out where he had gone. I'll always wonder about that little boy—who he was, what became of him and what could I have or should I have done?*

*My son and I talked for a long time. That more didn't happen was a relief. More would have, no doubt, if Denny had waited until I was safely in Mexico! My son seemed okay with me and happy to be away from Denny.*

*I contacted a family from church with a son in Ross' class and they happily took him in while I continued on to my vacation, a regret I carry with me still today.*

*Upon my return home, I was informed by the caregivers of my son that his dad hadn't waited until I came home to start some action. Denny was arrested and placed in jail in Denver. He'd bonded out and was with his brother. I was glad but surprised it'd all happened so fast.*

*Subsequently, Denny took his own life before being tried for his crimes, which were not his first. While confusing and difficult in its own right I'm grateful that it freed my son from any future fear of him.*

In case you don't believe this could ever happen to you, know that the lady in the story above is my own wife, and this happened after her divorce long before she and I met. She had her eyes open, she asked questions, and she believed her son. My point is that this can and does happen to people everywhere, so please be aware of this "grooming process."

*Theoren Fleury, the retired NHL star who won the Stanley Cup during his sixteen-year career in the Pro Hockey League and an Olympic Gold Medal with Team Canadian, described pedophiles in the act of grooming as "the greatest actors on our planet; they could be winners of Academy Awards .... Once they have a kid's trust, once they are in a position of power."*

*—Hollywood Reporter* (2009)

*It is estimated 1-5% [3,000,000 to 15,000,000] of the U.S. population molests children. A typical abuser is male, begins molesting by age 15 and will molest an average of 117 youngsters.*

—Dr. Gene Abel, CNN Specials
Transcript #454—Thieves of Childhood

## CHAPTER 6

# SEXUAL ABUSE IS EVERYWHERE

At the beginning, like most everyone else, I had no idea how many other people had been sexually abused; no idea whatsoever. And, furthermore, I had absolutely no interest in learning the soon-to-be-discovered huge numbers. I mean: why in the world would anyone have an interest and in tracking such a detestable subject?

Then, I started my own journey of discovery when the memories began returning, and I had to renege on my unconscious pact to never remember.

This is the intriguing insight to which I referred to at the end of chapter 3; an idea so eerie that it may perhaps perplex you as it did me.

When you buy a new car, you suddenly see the same model over and over. Or, when a woman becomes pregnant, she begins to notice more pregnant women than ever before. It's as if a magnet draws all these similar connections or one's perception becomes more keenly attuned to the similarities.

After my dream that gave me the title to this book, I requested a cover be designed to my specifications without any description as to what the book was about. The front cover was to be a picture of a weeping willow tree with only the words, EVEN THE TREES WERE CRYING, and my name, no mention of SA.

I began my normal procedure of soliciting feedback from people with whom I came into contact to see whether or not they were attracted to the cover. Responses were very positive. What I didn't expect was a response that came from three of the eight people I asked.

The first person I showed the cover to eagerly looked on before becoming transfixed; then suddenly, she started crying. I had not yet told her what the book was about.

When I reached out to her to give comfort, she began telling me about how she thinks one of her grandchildren was being sexually abused by another relative. After listening to her full story, I finally asked her, "How did you know the book was about sexual abuse?" Shaking her head, she replied, "I don't know. I just did."

Similar responses occurred with two other people, neither of them knew how they knew.

This is like the "We-were-checking-for-ringworm" responses that members of the pedophile group in prison proclaimed, almost in unison, when asked what they said if they were caught in a child's bedroom at night. Ironically, it's the same response/excuse my mother gave to me, justifying my father's actions in my bedroom; and, it's the same response Oprah Winfrey reported on one of her shows on SA. From these reactions and responses, my brain began formulating a strange and radical idea: *Was there some secret genetic code hiding in everyone and that only awakens, or is switched on, when in the presence of sexual abuse?*

This peculiar idea became only stronger as I continued writing this book and seeing other connections that had not been obvious before.

* * * * * *

Returning to my research of SA, I continued my journey and discovered more shocking data:

- One in four college students will experience rape during their supposedly carefree college days;

- The damage of SA affects the mental health of sixty million people in the U.S. alone;

- The similarities between child abuse and serial killers are shocking;

- Most abuse victims experience Post Traumatic Stress Disorder (PTSD) for the rest of their lives;

- Sexual abuse detrimentally affects a person's normal and healthy sexual development;

- The extent of the damages done by priests, coaches, medical doctors, and teachers (people in positions of trust) is unfathomable;

- Abuse victims regularly lose all self-esteem;

- A huge percentage of victims turn into drug and alcohol addicts;

- The vast majority of pedophiles have been sexually abused themselves, though only a small percentage of those who have been sexually abused become pedophiles.

This last fact eased my mind greatly as I often wondered why I have absolutely no interest in sexually abusing children, teenagers, or adults. Why not? I really can't answer this, only that I am eternally grateful that I don't and that I was able to bring to a halt this terrible behavior which has probably plagued my family tree for many generations.

Still undecided if I would return to finish this book (I had started some ten years earlier), one day my wife and I randomly stopped to see a friend at his office. Shockingly, my friend began unloading about a sudden change in his family. He explained that he and his wife were now taking care of three young children, relatives of his wife. The story was that both the mother and father were drug addicts, and the father had been sexually abusing the kids. He told us they had experienced evidence of the abuse firsthand when he had to keep stopping the brothers and sisters from *humping* each other. When he asked them where they learned the behavior, they were silent at first, until finally admitting it was "from our Daddy."

Then, my wife and I watched the motion picture on Netflix entitled *Spotlight*. Not aware of the movie's subject matter, I was again stunned as we discovered it was a true story about how the *Boston Globe* broke a story about the number of priests who had been abusing children in the Boston area.

The Boston diocese kept repeating the number of abuse cases involving priests represented a very small number. However, the *Boston Globe's* efforts disclosed the number of abusing priests eventually totaled 271 with over a thousand victims who *came forward.* And, in 2003, these *Boston Globe* articles received a Pulitzer Prize for Public Service for "its courageous comprehensive coverage … and effort that pierced secrecy, stirred local, national, and international reaction and produced changes in the Catholic Church."

So far, twelve Catholic dioceses have filed for bankruptcy and the Church paid about one billion dollars for the abuse claims in 2002—*Nation & World / News*, June 10, 2005.

These two seemingly random discoveries strongly

affirmed my need to finish the book—game on!

\* \* \* \* \* \*

You have probably read stories; seen some of the statistics; listened to prominent people such as Oprah Winfrey (one of the first highly visible celebrities to talk about their own SA) on her show openly discuss this subject; and surely you witnessed the notoriety of the Michael Jackson trial when he was accused of sexual abuse. SA finally began breaking out and exposing itself. This cunning depravity affects 60,000,000 people in our country and does more harm than the combined effects of all the diseases and accidents added together. Maybe, just maybe, cracking the denial of SA's existence is a step forward for the many victims.

Here are a few sample headlines that brought SA to the attention of the world although this represents the tip of the iceberg:

> ➤ "Abuse: Scandal Inquiry Damns Paterno and Penn State"—2012-07-2013, *New York Times.*

> ➤ "'Invisible War' exposes widespread rape

in U.S. Military"—2012-01-22, *Chicago Tribune.*

➤ "Vatican Declined to Defrock U.S. Priest Who Abused Boys"—2010-03-24, *New York Times.*

➤ "Pope 'Obstructed' sex abuse inquiry"—2005-04-24, *The Observer* (One of UK's leading newspapers.

➤ "Victorian police in pedophile rings: victims"—*Sydney Morning Herald* (One of Australia's leading newspapers).

➤ "Massive Pentagon Child Pornography Accusations Not Investigated"—2011-01-6, CNN.

➤ "Predator Priest Shuffled Around Globe"—2010-04-14, CBS News/Associated Press.

➤ "John Paul's Legacy Stained By Sex Abuse Scandal"—2015-04-21, ABC News/Associated Press.

➤ "Government Workers With Ties to Child Porn"—2012-09-19, *Forbes*

- ➢ "Recent Charges of Sexual Abuse of Children in Hollywood Just Tip of the Iceberg, Experts Say"—2011-12-05, Fox News.

- ➢ "Nebraska Inquiry Is Given File on Sex Abuse of Foster Children"—1988-12-25, *New York Times*.

- ➢ "Pope Francis: 'About 2% of Catholic clergy pedophiles'"—2014-07-13, BBC News.

- ➢ "The alleged pedophile ring at the heart of the British Establishment"—2014-07-06, *The Telegraph* (One of UK's leading newspapers).

- ➢ "Documents Reveal Decades of Child Abuse Among Some Chicago Priests"—2014-01-24, NPR.

- ➢ "Pope Conclave tainted by abuse scandal"—2013-03-05, *USA Today*.

Newspaper and magazine articles like these are prevalent throughout the world, and pedophiles and other sex abusers are found in every walk of life, e.g., priests and ministers; janitors and grocery clerks; MBAs and CEOs; teachers; television, movie, and radio stars. They are doctors, daddies, mommies, uncles .... The sheer numbers indicate they are everywhere.

Priests and doctors, however, have an almost inordinate amount of authority and power that puts them in a category by themselves; these positions have almost unfettered access to children and adults, who are taught to respect authority. This trust makes the acts of grooming easier.

As for *serial killers*, this one fact stands out: 100% of them had been abused as children (Journal of Police and Criminal Psychology, 2005, Volume 20, Number 1), whether through violence, humiliation, or neglect. It is estimated that one-third of the serial killers were physically abused, one-fourth sexually abused, and over fifty percent were psychologically abused.

Coaches are also categorized as persons who have greater power over their students than other members of society. An article from *USA Today Sports*, dated 8/4/2016, by Marisa Kwiatkowski, Mark Alesia, and Tim Evans directed our awareness to the fact that even in such a prominent organization as the Olympics, failure to report allegations of SA perpetrated by coaches occurred.

Furthermore, on 8/7/2016, I read an article in *USA Today* entitled "'Abysmal' track record on coaches.'" It began by stating that USA Gymnastics touts a list of coaches it had banned as a key safeguard to warn gym owners and parents about dangers of sexual predators to protect the young gymnasts. But an *Indianapolis Star* (2016/12/15) investigation uncovered example after example of coaches who were suspected of abuse and had actually been convicted of molestation; however, they did not show up on the banned coaches' list for years—even decades—after those convictions.

And, the stories go on ...

For example, when a pedophile pediatrician in Delaware was convicted and given a life sentence for sexually abusing his young patients, everyone was aghast that a once-admired doctor was capable of such brutal, horrifying acts.

Linda Ammons, a law school dean in Delaware told the AJC, December 9, 2011, "It is so hard to believe ... Everyone believes that the boogeyman is somebody you don't know, someone who is crouching in the dark bushes somewhere ... But that's not how it is. The boogeyman, 99 times of 100 is somebody you know, who you may respect and you may have had a long relationship with. That is just what we can't seem to get right."

The question remains, "If the magnitude, the preponderance of SA is so vast, *how in this world has such activity been allowed to persist?*"

*7% of girls' grades 5 through 8 will be sexually abused; 12% of girls' grades 9 through 12 will be sexually abused.*

—RAINN ((Rape, Abuse & Incest National Network)

CHAPTER 7

# THE ROLE OF DENIAL

Denial is another defense mechanism humans employ when internal or external realities are so unpleasant we prevent them from entering our conscious thinking. Denial is used by everyone and is often displayed by victims and families where SA takes place. Why? Because it is so gross and despicable that denial is easier than facing its existence.

Nearly always, when a family member garners the courage to verbally express they've been sexually abused (*especially* when the abuser is a family member or relative), the other family members, even if they, too, were sexually abused by the same abuser, will resort to denial.

For me, it took reaching the age of around fifty before I exposed the abuse to my primary family members. I told my mother, one sister and niece what had been happening to me by our husband/father/uncle. After my disclosure, while sitting around a kitchen table in Gunnison, Colorado where we were vacationing, it was like time had stopped. No one spoke a word. It was like my confession meant nothing; like both I and what had just been said were invisible and irrelevant. This was how I felt most of my life.

After departing shortly thereafter, I returned home, greatly disappointed because of the absence of support I received. Finally, two days afterwards, I called my one sister who had been present and asked why she didn't support me. Her response that followed was an unbelievable example of denial; it defied all logic and rationality. She retorted, "I don't believe you had been sexually abused by Dad. *I think you were abducted by UFOs and are confusing the situation!*"

Let me affirm that this beyond-absurd response came from a very intelligent person, and the therapists with whom I shared this poignant example were completely stunned despite working in the field of sexual abuse for many years.

I included this extreme example to show the insidious, Machiavellian, sly, cunning role denial plays in the context of SA. Unable to cope with the reality of SA, oftentimes, a person will revert to denial.

Living in Colorado, I remember reading in the *Denver Post* when Marilyn Van Derbur, the 1958 Miss America, made public her father's sexual abuse of her between the ages of five and eighteen. Her father was a very prominent Denver millionaire, businessman, and philanthropist. Marilyn's mother denied her assertion.

Then the city's denial spread throughout, including an article by a long-time *Denver Post* writer, Gene Amole, who boldly proclaimed Marilyn had to be lying. Only after Marilyn's sister confessed their father had also been sexually abusing her did the denial furor lose its credibility. Marilyn further asserted how incest survivors are ostracized by relatives and family friends when they had the courage to turn the guilty party in to the authorities. She explained that, when the victim finally garnered the courage to turn in a family member, they could expect to receive no help because they couldn't supply concrete proof it had occurred and their stories are received as preposterous.

Like most victims, Marilyn was plagued by doubters; even her mother proclaimed she had been *fantasizing.*

In the instance when I confronted my father and mother in a telephone call by asking my father, "What were you doing that night in California when I awoke to find you had pulled down the cover, my underpants, and were shining a light and touching my genitals?" Interestingly, my father said nothing. It was my mother who quickly responded, "Why, he didn't do that! You must have been dreaming."

Two weeks later, this was the incident where she called just to inform me he had been *checking for ringworm.*

To repeat what I wrote before: after reading about sexual abusers who participated in a study of pedophile prisoners, when asked what they said when caught in the middle of the night in a child's bedroom with the covers down, they all unanimously said, "We say we were checking for ringworm." How could this have occurred? How could this exact same excuse and even the exact wording be used by these predators? And, even my mother, who never sexually abused me, came to parrot these words? These questions are mind-boggling.

This discovery is similar to the earlier example where some people knew what was in this book only by looking at the cover and with no mention being made about sexual abuse. Is there some genetic code inside every human that holds the seed to this idea? This is a mystery that defies any rational explanation.

My own inability to remember the details of my own sexual abuse until around the age of thirty verifies the power of denial. Think about it; I had no lasting memories of the sexual abuse until a therapy session. I was just talking to the therapist when, out-of-the-blue, I said, "When I awoke at night and heard my father's knees creaking as he walked around the house, I always had the strange thought he was going to enter my room and *kill me*."

The therapist held the silence in the room until breaking it by whispering, "You thought your father was going to kill you? ...Why would you have a thought like that?"

Shaking my head in immediate denial, I said, "I don't know why. I mean, my father would never kill me ... would he?"

I never had such an idea before; it was only in the context of discussing it with a therapist that the thought became a permanent conscious memory.

Remember, denial is a defense mechanism individuals utilize when confronted with an internal or external reality that is so unpleasant we deny its existence. Certainly, it is deployed extensively to protect survivors of SA.

If someone told me a person whom I loved was a sex predator, what would I do? Would I deny it? Would I have the courage to have it stopped? Would I be like my mother and many other mothers throughout time who sold out the well-being of their children for the security of their marriage? Would I have the courage to confront a priest, coach, doctor, teacher, or community leader? There is no one face that represents a predator. They are literally in every facet of life, and they must be stopped by eradicating our denial and acting upon our increased awareness.

Why believe the children? Because 96% of the abuse claims are proved valid (*Philadelphia News and Opinion*, December 22, 2011).

Like the proverbial elephant in the living room, it will stay hidden and remain a large, ugly secret until we stand up and speak out; when more people begin recognizing the potential signs and symptoms; when we stop the denial and turning the blind eye.

I remember being seven or eight at my grandfather's farm with my parents. We were all watching television. Then, for no known reason, my father suddenly became angry and started making the sucking noise he made with his teeth and gums. Next, and for no apparent reason and certainly with no warning, he pulled a table into the middle of the room, stood me on the table, pulled down my pajamas and underwear and began *checking out my genitals*, all the while everyone else in the room grew deathly silent and tried not to look at what was happening. **And, no one ever said a thing**—not my mother, my grandfather, or my grandmother—all the while I stood on that small table with my pants down, engulfed in shame.

*3% of boys' grades 5 through 8 will be sexually abused; 5% of boys' grades 9 through 12 will be sexually abused.*

—RAINN ((Rape, Abuse & Incest National Network)

## CHAPTER 8

# A UNIQUE ODDITY OF SEXUAL ABUSE

Psychologically, one of the strangest offshoots of being sexually abused—one of the most illogical consequences—is that *the victim is the one who feels guilty and shamed!*

These feelings are also two of the most difficult to overcome because they defy logic and reasoning. I certainly had felt this way my whole life, even before the memories of SA returned. Even after being able to assign the cause of these feelings to the abuse acts, the guilt and shame persisted. Further recuperation required utilizing the EMDR and revised storytelling techniques I'll share later.

In my journey of healing, I came to understand

some of the effects of my SA:

- the perpetual fear that always resided within me; the constant presence of having to be vigilant at all times to possibly prevent the next event;

- nervousness, excessive sweating, ulcers, and both conscious and unconscious strong desire to kill myself or to somehow die;

- the aberrant feelings and sexual statements I blurted out at the most inappropriate times;

- though I wore *masks* that allowed me to *seem* normal, I had no idea who I was or how to act inside my skin;

- phases of voluntary vomiting to rid myself of food;

- depression;

- self-hatred;

- constant loneliness yet still desiring to be alone;

- drug usage; and,

- injuring myself.

I later learned to understand "why," but coming to terms with why guilt and shame were so deeply embedded in my psyche, I had no ideas as to the source. I was the victim, not the perpetrator.

*That is, until I came across this explanation: A child views their parents as gods; when that god does such horrible things to them, a child reasons the parent—or god—just couldn't be doing such a thing to them so they turn it inward and assume the responsibility for it.*

It also occurs in the abusing context with adults such as coaches, doctors, ministers, teachers, and priests. Children and young adults have already assigned them the power and authority as our society had taught them. Like their parents being gods, the same inward turning of guilt and shame takes place.

There is a difference between shame and guilt. *Guilt* mainly involves *others* and *shame* relates to *self.* Or, said differently, guilt is a feeling of remorse or responsibility for something one did, i.e., a crime or offense that is either real or imagined. Shame is the painful feeling in our consciousness because of some improper or dishonorable thing done by our self or by another—how we appear to others and/or ourselves but doesn't depend on us actually having done anything. Where there is a definite difference between the two, they often go hand-in-hand.

Guilt is probably more widely understood; shame is much more difficult and has a deeper impact. In fact, shame may be the major cause and is at the root of low-self-esteem. Simply understood, children and adults who feel shame feel bad about their own selves and, thus, adopt guilt and the belief they must have no worth. This, in turn, detrimentally affects their social skills and intimacy.

One of the oddest characteristics of shame is that there is no action a person can take that *releases* it. If one is sad, they can cry; if angry, perhaps shout. But, shame sticks like gum on the sole of your shoe, undermining so many areas of living while showing up as personality disorders, depression, great anxiety, and obsessive-compulsive disorders.

That is, until new healing methods emerged.

*One of the best kept secrets in America*
*is the sexual abuse of children.*

—Book by Florence Rush,
*The Best Kept Secret: Sexual Abuse of Children,*
Englewood Cliffs, N.J., Prentice Hall

## CHAPTER 9

# MEMORIES AND DREAMS

In the late Pat Conroy's book, *The Prince of Tides*, a novel about coming to grips in adulthood with childhood sexual abuse and rape, the main character and narrator spoke these haunting words, "Before I *chose not* to have the memories ...."

Seldom are dreams and memories fully coherent, linear remembrances. Often, they are fragmented, nonlinear bits of data that might come in flashes or maybe even in longer narratives filtered through a haze of personal perceptions, a kaleidoscope of feelings and words. How do you remember, in a way you can completely describe, the richness of a nightmare? How do you communicate the indescribable intricacies involved?

Of course, you can't. They are indecipherable, mysterious combinations of symbols and words known only to the one who experienced it.

The following is a true example, not a dream, of a metaphor attempting to portray actual settings in which I often found myself. Perhaps not indicative of any one situation but representing a collage of what had often actually taken place for me in my past. This is not from any dream but is a poetic attempt to convey the tense ambience I felt growing up in the Carwile family.

*Surrealistic. On holidays when no guests were present. Just family.*

*A bleak aura of fakery presided. Pretense without borders.*

*Only some physically palpable rage simmering in our midst.*

*Within one of us.*

*I felt—believed—if I could only peddle fast enough, things would be okay. And many times, they were kept contained.*

*But remembrances of times past ... times*

138

*when things weren't*
  *contained ... permeated every occasion,*
*awaited in the dark*
  *to lurch out in violence.*

*The volcano might erupt suddenly, out of*
*nowhere, shattering our fakery*
  *of peace or, the tension might simmer*
*under the surface,*
  *bubbling slowly. Building in intensity.*
*Unstoppable. Unpreventable.*

*No doubt, the simmering feelings were*
*easier to take. Then, at least,*
  *you had time to prepare, even though past*
*explosions always lingered in*
  *the back recesses of your mind like an*
*impending dog bite.*
  *Always waiting ... Expectant ... Ominous.*

*While some members of our seemingly*
*happy-to-the-outside-world*
  *family pretended things were hunky-dory;*
*this little façade left me with*
  *realistic memories isolated in a fog of*
*loneliness and fear.*

*Unstable and fragile. Believing deep inside
that I must somehow be the
cause—that "it" must derive from my own
misperceived sinfulness.*

Memories are like that sometimes.

If three people observe a criminal fleeing the scene, oftentimes, there will be three different descriptions of the fleeing party. Attorneys are very aware that an eye witness is among the least reliable of accurate evidence.

Like in a fog, we see, dimly, only vague images filtered through our past experiences, only random glimpses snatched from brief miniscule remembrances, leaving one vexed and disappointed until the fog, once again, disappears leaving one feeling as if lost at sea.

They say you're only as healthy as your darkest secrets, meaning the more completely you can bring these secrets out into the light, the healthier you'll be. You might ask, "But, what if these secrets hold too much pain and suffering? Is it better, safer, to sometimes not delve too deeply in one's past?"

The answer is a *definitive "no"* because only with the light can there be healing. Not exploring one's full self will only enhance the yearning to know; it is as if there is an innate desire for all beings to piece back together their whole selves. Like scattered pieces of a puzzle, we all seek full knowledge of who we are. The healer and author, Carolyn Myss, captures the essence of this point in an illustration. She says it is as if a perfect crystal ball is dropped at the instant a person is born, shatters and each person's life task is to find all the pieces.

It's kind of like when you push a beach ball down under the water and it slips from your grasp. The beach ball does *not* come straight up but erupts out of the water at different angles. It is the same for your secrets. Despite your efforts to keep your fears and secrets hidden—in the dark—at some point, they will pop up at unexpected times and places.

Without bringing all aspects of yourself into the light, including your dark sides, each new day will begin under the cloud. You will still possess some inner yearnings to know what is contained within. Some days you might feel okay, maybe even great, yet still sensing, expecting the next shooting star might release that small seed of some horrific memory—stark and windless, deflating your sails, erasing all sense of hope.

These are the metaphors of my memories and dreams. Yet, they leave me pondering an eternal question: how do you differentiate magnified memories from reality? How can you know what is real and what is not?

*15 of 16 rapists/sexual assault abusers
will walk free.*

—U.S. Department of Justice Statistics

## CHAPTER 10

# ALL FORMS OF ABUSE ARE DESTRUCTIVE

The main focus of this book is sexual abuse; however, I want to make it crystal clear that all *emotional* and *physical* abuse is highly destructive. Each type is abhorrent; each deteriorates the human spirit in its own unique way; and most, if not all of us, experience/respond to each in various ways.

For me, personally, many instances of emotional and physical abuse come to mind, often at unpredictable times. There does not seem to be any rhyme or reason for when the memories return though I am blind in this area of psychology because of my closeness to the events. Their numbers seem endless, but these three memories stand out most vividly:

The first happened when I was nine years old and on a duck-hunting trip alone with my father. We were on Matagorda Island off the coast of Texas, an island partially owned by the Air Force to be used solely by Air Force personnel supposedly.

Just prior to sunrise, my father and I had crawled behind a sand dune to wait until sunrise, the legal time to begin shooting. We could hear with certainty that some ducks had landed nearby but had no idea how many. He instructed me to aim at only one duck at a time and not point randomly.

We watched as the gorgeous morning sunrise began spreading along the sandy beach. When he yelled, "Now!" we both quickly stood up only to discover that not just a few ducks had landed, but actually thousands.

For me, the sight of the flaming orange sunrise coupled with the flapping wings of countless ducks all rising at the same time proved too beautiful a scene, for I found myself unable to shoot; I could only stand in awe.

At some point, my consciousness heard him angrily screaming, "Shoot! Shoot, goddamn it!"

Then I felt his wrath. He knocked me down, cursed, and kicked me repeatedly. (This was from a father who supposedly loved me.)

The second memory involved baseball. As a kid growing up on military bases, my fondest memories centered on the sport; I played every day the weather allowed and became quite good. When I was ten years old, the family moved to the island of Guam and I joined organized baseball for the first time.

Unaware of my talents and playing with teammates two years older, I zoomed to the top of my team and the league in both fielding and hitting. Promoted to first-team third baseman, I found my batting average soared to over .500. The game was a natural for me; it felt as if it was what I had been created to do.

But then, my father, under the guise of making me an even better player, took over coaching the team and, under his tutelage, he literally destroyed my skills within weeks. During the third game of my second season, after poor hitting and many fielding errors, I was removed and benched.

His constant screaming, cursing, and berating

me had taken its toll. I could no longer even catch nor hit the ball.

I recall, shortly thereafter, one of the other coaches who had, at first, admired my talents and had observed what my father had been doing to me, came up after I had been removed from first string, put his arm around my shoulders and whispered with a grim face, "I'm so sorry for you, young man."

Where was my mother during all this public abuse? She was meekly and cowardly sitting in the stands, watching it all and just like with the sexual abuse, never saying a word or doing a thing to stop it. I must confess that I do still have disappointment and anger over the cowardly way my mother dealt with my father's degrading behavior towards me. Certainly she must have been frightened herself of his terrible rages and was too weak to stand up to him for her own self, but I do strongly believe she should have broken out of her fear to at least protect her child.

The third memory involved hunting doves and is much more complicated.

To begin, I need to affirm that I was an excellent shot and was always extremely cautious around firearms from having attended many National Rifle Association safety courses.

We had just arrived at the dove field. Of course, my father had been criticizing me unmercifully about something during the ride. Getting out of the car first, he crossed over to my side still ragging on me. I remember exiting the car, loading a live shotgun shell into the chamber and, mysteriously, having no memory of actually doing it, I fired the gun and watched as the pattern of BBs narrowly missed his head.

I cannot repeat strongly enough that, at the time, I was mortified and mystified how the gun had gone off. Pale-faced and shocked, my father's berating of me stopped. After taking a few minutes to compose himself, he said only, "Get in. We're going home." I felt terrible and still wonder to this day how it had happened.

In retrospect, I came to see quite clearly how my subconscious was trying to save me by killing him. Following this episode, I often speculated how my life would have been had those little BB's found their karmic target.

Reliving that scene many, many times, I so

wished I had the clarity and strength on that trip home to lean over and quietly, but firmly, whisper, "If you ever again scream at me, berate or do what you've been doing to me in my bedroom at night, the next time I'll shoot your balls off."

Certainly, all of us have had bad memories from our parents' or guardians' abuses and short-comings. But, whether mild or horrific, *all abuse takes its toll* on each victim's life and, then, on society collectively.

Perhaps, however, the worst effect of all forms of abuse can be summarized in, again, that one word—*shame!*

Many highly influential psychologists specu-late that shame may very well be the *root of low self-esteem*: simply said, shame makes us feel bad about who we are. Perhaps we are born into this world in a state of perfection with intrinsically high self-worth, and then it is parental influences (often inherent from their own life experiences) and soci-etal pressures that begin chipping away at these wondrous creatures we are.

Burdened by shame, a young person may begin developing a pattern of being uncomfortable in social situations preventing the development of healthy social skills and intimacy. This leads to having only superficial relationships, seeking isolation, feeling loneliness, and a decimation of creativity and curiosity. These characteristics then lead to fits of extreme anger and hostility. To cover up the shameful feelings, a person may hide behind attitudes of bullying, project false feelings of superiority, and feel the necessity of having to dominate every situation.

These mannerisms are also predictable for the sexually abused although the inner rage may express itself in outward anger and drug usage, self-mutilation, sexual perversions or a multitude of other self-destructive effects. If you have not been sexually abused or raped (especially by a family member), you would find it totally impossible to comprehend the confusion and convoluted thinking one must deal with. The unjustified guilt and shame that go with the territory literally destroys all sense of self-worth. Almost every day, you are haunted with such despair and darkness that most of your efforts are put towards just trying to act normal.

I cannot emphasize my next point strongly

enough: While there are, most definitely, varying degrees of sexual abuse that occur, whether your experience was one of the worst cases OR if your sexual abuse was only *mild*, or happened only once, any sexual abuse makes you a member of this club no one wants to be a member of. You may very well exhibit many of the same dysfunctional physical, emotional, and sexual effects as the victim who experienced the most horrid.

I remember being asked to attend a meeting normally limited to only men who were working as therapists and had been sexually abused themselves. After one of the men, a rather large and muscular man, had described one of his disturbingly abusive incidents, the room fell silent. It was then that one of the other participants meekly spoke up and said that, perhaps, he shouldn't be a part of the group because his abuse was comparatively mild. The only uncomfortable thing his mother did to him was lie on top of him and lick and suck his nipples!

With tears in his eyes, the gentleman who had earlier shared his horrible experience boldly stated, "My friend, trust me on this one, you belong here just as much as I do."

Regardless of the type of abuse you experienced, do not give up. There is more than just hope; there are some new, as well as tried and true psychological techniques that actually work; proven methods that can return your life to normalcy, like sunshine breaking through the clouds.

*1 in 4 women will experience sexual
assault on campus.*

—*The New York Times,* September 21, 2015

## CHAPTER 11

# MY REAL-LIFE NIGHTMARE CONTINUES

The year was 2000. As my severe and chronic back and spine pain had returned in full force over the previous five years, and every day was focused primarily on pain management, I reached the end of my physical and emotional tolerance. With great reservation, I informed my then sixteen-year-old daughter of the possibility of my committing suicide because of the ever-present pain. I feebly attempted to assure her that suicide would not be a part of her life legacy or personal experience. (Looking back, it is quite obvious how mentally unstable I was at the time). But first, I chose to take one last trip to visit the Florida Keys—a place I had read about most of my life but had never visited.

Before my declaration of suicide, I had met a woman whom I had come to think of as a friend at a seminar in California on personal growth. She and I had maintained contact through telephone conversations while I was still using cocaine quite heavily. When I expressed my intent to visit the Florida Keys, she immediately responded that I should first fly to Bonita Springs, Florida, where she lived, which was just north of the Keys, and we could drive together.

It sounded like a good idea, so I did. Unfortunately, we were only two days into our trip when she took it upon herself to enter my room and remove her robe. Our sexual relationship began way too soon and with very little firm ground beneath us to support it.

Three facts are important to know: she was aware of my current mental condition (and my healthy financial balance sheet, by the way), she was a trained psychotherapist (had studied at the Carl Jung Institute in Zurich, Switzerland); and she was financially broke herself, a fact she lied about after telling me she had $100,000 that she could contribute towards possibly buying a condo together in Naples. These factors set the stage for me to be manipulated and seduced (I would never have been susceptible to this if I had been in a healthy state of mind). I saw her as my only hope. Then, with me as an ordained minister, we married only three months later—I performed the marriage ceremony, just the two of us present in the living room of the house I owned. This all occurred to the chagrin and dismay of my daughter, her closest friends (whom I knew well), and my own friends. My new wife and I then moved to Naples, Florida.

To say the relationship was like a rocky rollercoaster ride would be an understatement. Despite the continued questioning from my friends regarding the possibility that she had married me for my money, I could only look upon her as my last and only source of hope. This desperate hope persisted despite her admitting she had lied about many things, including the before-stated fact she had $100,000 to contribute. Her deep-seated anger and acute jealousy flared up frequently during the brief marriage, twice confessing to me she even "had thoughts of killing" me. Shocked, I asked her why. She responded she was "just projecting my anger at my own parents and not to worry as this is the safest relationship I have ever been in!" Her justification buoyed me up, again, but, I can see clearly in hindsight, that if I had been in a healthier mental state, I would have left the relationship pronto after hearing that shocking admission.

Finally, three months after arriving in Florida, an incident occurred that shattered my blindness. We had an argument over why I would not lie concerning her idea to publicly advertise that her therapeutic skills had totally cured our housekeeper's psychological problems. She had wanted to use this example to start her own psychological counseling service in Naples. Not agreeing to this farcical marketing hope of hers, I opened my eyes to her other lies and deceits and somehow it all crystallized for me. I informed her I would not go along with such an absurdity.

My rejection of her idea eventually erupted in the bedroom later in the afternoon when she exploded into a rage and verbally attacked me. Then, suddenly, getting off the bed in an angry fit, I thought she was going for the shotgun I kept under the bed for protection from a possible break-in. (This was a family trait we learned from our father, and both my sisters and I always had a gun readily available near the bed.) Beating her to it, I unsheathed the shotgun, ejected the shells from it, then handed it to her and said, "Now you can have the goddamn gun."

She walked out of the room, leaving me standing alone. I looked down at the ejected shells lying on the bed and suddenly saw all of her lies clearly and remembered her statements that she had thoughts of killing me and I felt like a complete fool for allowing this to go on for so long. I yelled to her, "I'm calling 9-1-1 and heard her running down the stairs and slamming the front door. Presuming she was fleeing, I informed the 9-1-1 operator that I thought my wife had tried to kill me and was told to wait for the police to arrive.

I had no idea that instead of running from the scene, she had driven to the security gate, waited for the police to arrive and then, apparently with great theatrics, convinced them I was the culprit. When the police arrived at our condo, I had begun "dissociating." Sitting on the floor dazed, vague, and lethargic, they immediately said I was the one who was going to be arrested because she was the one who had been much more *visibly upset*. It turns out that it was police policy that one of the couple had to be taken into custody. As they were handcuffing me, I was stunned and could only mumble, "I can't believe this—I thought I had done the right thing by calling you."

Never jailed before, much less handcuffed, I found the whole experience humiliating and degrading—the same characteristics I had endured most of my life. After being locked up, I quickly learned from other prisoners that, to get out, I had to post bail, which I was able to do the following afternoon using my credit card. Next, I took a taxi to the bank for money to cover my credit card charge only to discover she had cleaned out both of my checking accounts and safety deposit box of over $130,000, leaving me broke, except for my credit cards. Luckily, I had not added her to them as a cosigner.

The attorney I found from the bail bondsman's recommendation soon called me with the surprise news that my wife's new attorney had contacted him with the offer that she would leave town and not testify against me if I would sign over all the money she had taken from the bank. Though scared to death over the possibility of going to jail, I still quickly stated and without any forethought, "No way in the world would I do that. I haven't done anything wrong."

Despite the obvious evidence of her immediately cleaning out the bank account, her offer to leave town, and the recording of my 9-1-1 call, it was strongly recommended to me by *four attorneys* to see if the courts would allow me to plead down from the felony charges to a misdemeanor. The two primary reasons all four attorneys gave me were simple: because of the public's preordained belief that the male is always the responsible party in any family dispute and, more to the point, this was the post O.J. Simpson era. Plus, I discovered the shocking and unknown-to-me fact about our legal system—*over 95% of all cases in our good old U.S. of A. are pled down to a lesser charge!* (Bureau of Justice Assistance, U.S. Department of Justice, January 24, 2011.)

The final result of this fiasco, after great, great resistance and doubting, was that I accepted a temporary felony domestic violence conviction.

However, after completing all of the requirements, I was released from probation in less than two years. Furthermore, the court withheld adjudication and changed the record to show it as only a *misdemeanor*. The receipt of this plan came about because I had no prior history of violence.

What I eventually learned from this experience was this:

First, I came to clearly realize that, in my depressed state of mind, I had subconsciously *chosen* to be in another situation that would leave me degraded and humiliated.

The second, and believe it or not, actually resulted in a tremendously beneficial aspect—I came to understand what PTSD (Post Traumatic Stress Disorder) was, and I had been experiencing it, off and on, all my life.

Third, and also of great benefit, was my realization that I needed medical help for my depression. Additionally, my drinking had accelerated to a half-gallon of alcohol a day. Fortunately, I had a doctor friend in Florida who was aware of my past sexual abuse history and readily called in a prescription for antidepressants, a much-needed drug I should have been on most of my life.

I returned to Denver suffering from PTSD and severe depression; the medication had not yet kicked in (it usually takes two to four weeks). I was as confused and lonely as I had ever been—barely able to function. But, it was here I stumbled upon something more helpful than anything I had found before. Another friend of mine was subleasing a portion of her office space to a therapist from Boulder, Colorado, who had worked with sexual abuse and trauma patients using a relatively little unknown technique, EMDR, one I had only recently heard about despite all my past research on healing.

*One of the greatest secrets of all times ... is that every adversity brings with it a gift.*

—Albert Einstein

# Book 2

# The Trial of the Century

*In one study, 98% of males who raped boys*
*were reported to insist that they were*
*heterosexual and not homosexual.*

—"Sexual Abuse of Boys", *Journal of the American Medical Association*, December 2, 1998

## CHAPTER 12

# THE MICHAEL JACKSON TRIAL

*Most people walk around half asleep … and there's
a rumor going around that a few might even wake up.*

—attributed to author C.S. Lewis

There was another event in my life that, once
again, dramatized the fact that our society is in
such denial about sexual abuse's prevalence that
we continue to choose blindness rather than expose
this epidemic. We opt to walk around in a dream
rather than wake up so we can admit its destructive
force and eradicate it.

Along came the Michael Jackson trial with accusations of him being a pedophile.

\* \* \* \* \* \*

Every once in a long while, as our society plods along in its blindness, as if asleep, a crack occurs in our perception, light gnaws its way out of the darkness and a once deeply buried evil secret is revealed—a myth is shattered and truth comes shining forth as bright as any star. America missed one of its best opportunities to do two major things with the Michael Jackson trial: one, to disclose sexual abuse's vast numbers and, second, to ignite the process of eradicating it from our society.

In case you may have forgotten, or didn't have an interest in following the coverage, mega pop star Michael Jackson was brought to trial in case #1133603: The People of the State of California v. Michael Joseph Jackson in 2005. When a 13-year-old boy named Gavin Arviso accused Jackson of sexual abuse and Jackson was indicted on four counts of molesting a minor, four counts of intoxicating a minor to molest him, one count of attempted child molestation, and one count of conspiring to hold the boy and his family captive at his 2700-acre Neverland Ranch. He was also charged with conspiring to commit extortion and child abduction.

The seated jury consisted of four men and eight women. These twelve ordinary people would decide the fate of one of the biggest and most successful musical performers in the world. Twenty-two hundred reporters covered the trial—more than the O.J. Simpson and Scott Peterson trials totaled together.

You may have heard the expression "the shot heard around the world." Well, in this case, it was the "trial," literally, heard around the world for it held the potential to expose a sexual problem that was, and still is, being kept a secret despite its sixty million victims in the U.S. This kind of abuse is so hideous that abusers persistently deny its existence, and our whole society, too often, denies it to the degree they often stand behind the abuser in support. Our past reveals that victims who do come forward are usually shunned and debased for their accusations and may even be fired from their jobs, depending on the situation. Because they have no physical proof except for their own personal testimonies, who would believe them when their accusers were seemingly good people, staunch citizens, family members, active in their churches and communities? Who could believe that one human would denigrate another person so horribly?

Out of the blue, I received a call from a lady in Sacramento, California, who had read my first book, *The Storyteller 1*, and requested that I read some of her poetry. After e-mailing me twelve of her poems, it was clear this lady, who taught twelfth-grade English, had talent. I typed the acknowledgment to her and assumed I wouldn't hear from her again.

Two weeks later, I received another e-mail from her with another request: *Would I co-author a book with her on the Michael Jackson trial ... her grand-mother was juror #5!* She further explained that her grandmother would be able to tell us what actually took place in the jury room; the inside scoop, so to speak.

Stunned, my first internal reaction was to readily accept. What followed next, though, was the fear that exposing myself into this dark subject matter (of SA) might further my depression. After much thought, I politely declined. She tried twice more to convince me ... until I finally capitulated.

Little did I know—did any of us know—the effects of my decision. The story that we were writing the book somehow broke in an article by Stuart Pfeifer, a reporter for the *Los Angeles Times*. Calling me direct to confirm certain information, especially if juror #5 was disclosing information about what was going on in the jury room while the trial was still ongoing, I assured him I had not received any inside information and did not even know juror #5's name.

Immediately following the first call from *The Los Angeles Times* writer, I was called by an *Associated Press* reporter, Tim Malloy, who asked questions similar to those of the first reporter. His article was then reprinted by many newspapers throughout the U.S. and the world, which instigated a whirlwind of actions for my wife and me.

Shortly after this, and while returning from a visit with friends in the Colorado Rocky Mountains I received my next surprise call from CNN; an Eric Spinato, who worked for the Paula Zahn show. Surprised at how he had obtained my unlisted *cell number*, he confidently replied, "I have my sources."

After arriving home, I found a call from *Good Morning America's* producer, Tarana Harris, on my home telephone's voice mail. She first tactfully praised my book, *The Storyteller 1*, and then asked me to appear on the show immediately following the jury's decision. While talking it over with my wife, Tarana quickly called back and wanted me on the show even before the jury's decision: could my wife and I fly from Colorado to San Francisco that evening?

That we did and from that moment on, Mary and I were on an exhilarating runaway train, holding onto our seats. Following the *Good Morning America* filming and spending a beautiful day in San Francisco complete with sumptuous dinner supposedly courtesy of GMA, (but who never reimbursed us for the bill), we were awakened the next morning at our San Francisco hotel at 6:30 a.m. to be picked up and taped for an episode on *Court T.V.*

Honestly, I must admit this part of the whole deal, being picked up at airports by limousines, first-class flight accommodations, staying at a 4-star hotel in San Francisco, and dining in the finest restaurants proved to be luxurious and ego-gratifying. On our return to Denver, thinking the furor would die down, we were surprised over and over as invitations poured in for interviews on the local T.V. networks and news media in Denver.

It was definitely a real kick, but keep in mind, all this happened and I had not yet written a single word.

\* \* \* \* \* \*

My earlier decision to co-author this book about Michael Jackson and his "alleged" SA came only after much soul-searching. I recalled again the first sentence in Scott Peck's book, *The Road Less Traveled,* which said, "Life is difficult." These simple words were what empowered me to agree to write, thus counteracting my fear that delving back into the subject matter would drag me down into the dreaded depression.

Then, I recalled two other very significant events that occurred in our history that had been hugely successful in effecting massive change. Like awakening from a dream, these two happenings seemed to startle us out of our denials so we could see them clearly for what they were.

One of the events was the formation of **MADD: "Mothers Against Drunk Driving."**

Formed in 1980 by Candace Lightner, a mother whose daughter was killed by a drunk driver, Ms. Lightner later discovered the same driver had been arrested earlier for a hit-and-run DUI. She became so irate over our society's loose regulations on **drunk driving**—look-the-other-way law enforcement and the near universal belief that drunk driving was socially acceptable—she set out to break through this veil, this false myth, by initiating a program of educating our world to its dangers. It was her tireless efforts that resulted in the establishment of lower blood alcohol standards of .08% or higher and the ensuing mandatory jail sentences for offenders.

Flashback: remember, not too long ago, how it seemed everyone would go out for cocktails with friends, consume too much alcohol, get behind the wheel and barely make it home by having to squint with just one eye open to help improve one's clarity of sight. Remember how later we all would laugh and joke about their poor driving ability while intoxicated? This was normal behavior for our society; it was acceptable behavior. That is, until Candace Lightner began her crusade. She became so vocal, so get-in-your-face with this very dangerous and deadly attitude and commonplace occurrence that she eventually broke through society's denial. Our entire world changed because of it.

Today, because of her and her organization's actions and the resulting changed laws from their insistence, almost everyone now clearly understands and knows that not only is drinking and driving highly dangerous for everyone, but it is also illegal with quite detrimental penalties.

The second portentous event and awakening occurred when **the dangers of tobacco and second-hand smoke** were revealed. Picture the romantic image of our movie stars sucking on a cigarette in nearly every picture show. Visualize the proliferation of advertisements on the life enhancements cigarette-smoking brings. Remember the rugged portrayal of the Marlboro man, riding his horse into the West? Then, note the percentage of smokers in the U.S. soaring to a high of 42%— smokers who were not only killing themselves but many were ending their lives with great suffering and pain. And, that Marlboro Man with the macho man image? He himself died a horrible death from lung cancer.

Similar to drinking and driving, most people intuitively sensed that smoking was bad for their health, but because almost everyone was doing it, perhaps they rationalized it really wasn't so bad. Look at all those movie idols who smoked: Humphrey Bogart, Yul Brenner, Mel Gibson, Bette Davis, John Wayne, and even Doris Day. Why, if they smoked, it can't be bad for us, can it?

Remember how you initially felt after taking your first puff off a cigarette and inhaling it? Or, the dizziness felt afterwards? Yet, somehow being wrapped up in the "smoking is cool" myth, as if we were walking around asleep in a state of denial, we kept puffing away on those cancer sticks thinking we were chic. All the while, our bodies were being impregnated with an array of cancerous products.

The Surgeon General had been trying to expose the destructiveness of smoking for years, but the tobacco industry's lobbying efforts were too strong, revealing that money often wins over health and common sense.

Then, two major discoveries occurred that finally cracked open the smoking myth. These events were the result of disclosures by these men:

Merrill Williams and Jeffrey Wigand. What these two individuals did would profoundly transform the *entire tobacco industry* in the United States by *illegally* providing documents that showed the tobacco industry lied in three major areas and, in fact, cigarette smoking *does* cause cancer; nicotine is addictive; and they *were* marketing to kids.

First, Merrill Williams was a paralegal for Wyatt Tarrant & Combs, a legal firm in Louisville, Kentucky that did work for Brown & Williamson, the third largest tobacco company in the U.S. His job was to work in the document room at Brown & Williamson, specifically to code all internal records and research findings that might be used by anti-smoking organizations' efforts to sue the tobacco companies. Some of the codes he was instructed to use included "DDA" for lung cancer, "DA" for addiction, "DDB" for throat cancer, "DDC" for other cancers and "DDE" for permanent genetic damage (can you believe this?).

Sometime along the way, Williams realized the whole purpose of his work was to "cover up" the destruction that Big Tobacco was wreaking on smokers. Stunned, he came to the uncomfortable conclusion the only ethical decision was one that was *illegal*. Despite this, he still made the decision to pursue the disclosure by making copies of over 4,000 pages of internal documents at Brown & Williamson and then releasing these damning documents to the public. He became a whistle-blower.

Following this action, one year after these documents had been revealed, the second man, Jeffrey Wigand, added gasoline to this already explosive disclosure. Wigand, a vice-president for research for Brown & Williamson from 1989 to 1993 was initially hired to work on the development of less harmful cigarettes. One year later, he was informed the program had been scrapped although he would remain employed.

Over the next two years, he made startling discoveries—the company already knew tobacco was habit-forming and was engineering its tobacco products to become even more addictive by adding substances they knew were seriously harmful to any living creature. After his discoveries, he wrote a memo delineating his findings to CEO Thomas E. Sandefur. The result: he was fired for "difficulty in communicating."

After discovering that Merrill Williams had

released the secret 4,000 documents that corrobo-
rated his findings, Wigand agreed to a world-shat-
tering disclosure interview on *60 Minutes*, and then
to testify in a Mississippi anti-tobacco lawsuit. He
never would have guessed he and his families' lives
would be threatened as a result, including finding a
bullet in their mailbox.

The actions of these two individuals plainly
professed to the world that tobacco companies had
been poisoning people for years. They also uncovered the depth of greed and corruption.

\* \* \* \* \* \*

Breaking through our consciousness, these two
disturbing disclosures brought light into two areas
of our societies' thinking; that where before we
had been in the dark, now these two false beliefs
would forever alter our perceptions of *driving after
drinking* and *smoking cigarettes*.

\* \* \* \* \* \*

I hope you understand these two stories vividly
depict how we, as a society, choose to stick our heads
in the sand when something is reprehensible rather

than face up to its existence and eradicate it.

Because of what I discovered concerning these two courageous acts, I found the guts to say yes to writing about the Michael Jackson trial.

I realized this trial represented a microcosm of our society, one that fosters an environment for SA and how it impels people to being so embarrassed they close their eyes to it. Therefore, I decided its disclosure might make us ask the difficult questions: Which ones of us are the pedophiles? How can we protect our children from the evil Boy Scout leaders, pedophile priests, deviant ministers, doctors, coaches and, worst of all, deranged pedophile parents and relatives?

\* \* \* \* \* \*

Having an insider in the jury (Juror #5), we now have the opportunity to go inside the inner workings of a trial and see, firsthand, the real story of how the jury found Michael Jackson innocent despite all the evidence. How did we, as a society, lose the potential for eradicating SA?

*The Michael Jackson trial could have been the catalyst for invoking a huge shift in our thinking, awakening us to the self-defeating practices around the secrecy and denial of sexual abuse.*

*93% of juvenile sexual assault victims*
*knew their attackers.*

—Department of Justice, Office of Justice Programs, Bureau of Justice Statistics, Sexual Assault of Young Children as Reported to Law Enforcement (2000)

CHAPTER 13

# INSIDE THE JURY ROOM OF THE MICHAEL JACKSON TRIAL

We know the Michael Jackson trial ended with a verdict of *not guilty*. We also know he had four previous SA claims against him, which were settled out of court and presumed to include settlement monies. For myself, after reading most of the court documents and testimonies, I personally concluded that, *in my opinion*, he was a sexual predator and abuser. Therefore, the sixty-four-thousand-dollar question would have to be—how did he get off scot-free? As juror #5, Ellie Cook proclaimed, "He was guilty as sin, but is free as a bird."

The only way to understand this juxtaposition, this oxymoron, would be to observe what went on in that jury room. Like a fly on the wall, through juror # 5's recounting, you will discover what actually went on.

\* \* \* \* \* \*

Immediately following the decision and release of the jury, my wife and I flew to Sacramento, California, rented a car, and drove to the granddaughter's (Traci M.) home where the interviews would be conducted. This would only be the second time I had met Traci and the first time to meet the juror #5, Ellie Cook. After our initial introductions, I pulled out my tape recorder and began with the first questions.

Ernie: "Ellie, why did the jury find Michael Jackson (from now on, we'll use the initials MJ) not guilty?"

Ellie: "Because most of the jurors believed he was innocent even before they heard any testimony. They were never going to change their minds ... they were never going to convict him right from the get-go.

They said things like, 'Oh, Michael wouldn't do such a thing ... I mean this is Michael Jackson!'"

Ellie went on to explain it was her feeling that this was the mindset at least nine of the jurors entered the jury room with and would hold on to come hell or high water.

Ernie: "What was the first count by the jurors as to MJ's innocence or guilt?

Ellie: "The first vote was 9 innocent, 3 guilty."

Ernie: "What happened to get the other three to change, including you? What changed their minds?"

Ellie: "Pressure. Why, I felt it so strongly from the others. And when the other two felt enough pressure, they caved in even though I still held onto my belief in his guilt."

Ernie: "Was the pressure really that strong?"

Ellie: "Oh man, they even tried to get me kicked off the jury because I wouldn't agree with everyone else. It became actually scary for me. I felt threatened."

I interviewed her over the next five days, grilling her with question after question and heard again and again that the initial tone and overall mindset of the other jurors predominated. While Ellie kept going back to the pressure she felt all along for her belief in his guilt, I kept thinking of the book, *The Lord of the Flies*, and how a group of young boys stranded on an island become killers of any of their members who don't go along with the leader and the other boys. The author, William Golding, conveyed how individuals in any society form together and make rules that must be followed and all members must obey the leaders. The same concept played out in this jury room.

Ernie: "Why did you finally capitulate and vote 'not guilty?'"

Ellie: "Well, I certainly didn't think I was going to convince them to vote the way I believed, so I just got tired of having to fight with everyone."

Ernie: "Do you believe he was guilty?"

Ellie: "Guilty as sin!"

I remembered thinking to myself that, once again, another myth will stay hidden in the shadows. I believe most people trust that our justice system is honest and true. However, I heard with my own ears this is another falsehood; that our justice system does not always depict the truth but is tainted by each juror's own biases and prejudices. Having read many of the trial's transcripts, I easily came to the conclusion MJ was guilty even though I, too, held MJ's musical talents in high esteem.

From my research, I discovered that no big entertainment figure had been convicted of a murderous crime, e.g., O.J. Simpson, Robert Blake, and Fatty Arbuckle. Somehow, these people have strong and influential personas that prevent, perhaps, ordinary people from convicting them of murder.

MJ was not a case of murder but of sexual abuse, and I believe there were *two* main factors that brought about his innocent verdict. One, his being such a famous, influential, and talented mega pop star had to color the jurists.

The second overwhelming cause of a not-guilty verdict may have been the result of SA being so repugnant to a normal person to even conceive such an act could occur. SA is a cultural taboo in every society. Because it is so unbelievably nasty, we prefer to *deny* its existence to the extent of protecting the abuser and denigrating the accuser.

This trial held the power to bring SA into the light and eradicate this perversion perpetrated on innocent victims. But, **unlike** the realizations that drunk driving and smoking are harmful, our society chose blindness—stay asleep and pretend it doesn't exist!

*"A man was walking in a park on a beautiful summer day,*

*the smells of fresh-mowed grass permeating the air, the*

*perfume from flowers omnipresent.*

*"The large park possessed a central lake with a walking path*

*circling it. Blissfully enjoying the scenery and splendor,*

*he happened to notice a group of people had gathered around a lone man who seemed to be speaking to them. Too far away to*

*hear exactly what was being told to the group, it was easy to*

*surmise that it must have been of great importance as everyone*

*present seemed to be mesmerized.*

*"Angling towards the group, just as he arrived, he observed that*

*everyone had gone completely silent, until finally one lady called*

*out, 'Are you some kind of prophet?' to which the speaker said,*

*The speaker said, 'Absolutely, not.'*

*"Then a man called out, 'Are you a magician or mind reader?'*

*The man sadly shook his head again, 'No.'*

*"Finally, someone called out, 'Then what are you?'*

*This time the man spoke very precisely and clearly and said,*

*'I ... am ... awake.'"*

Can you see that sexual abuse represents another blindness in our world? Like the ideas that smoking is bad for our health and driving while intoxicated is highly dangerous, sexual abuse will continue until we awaken from this sleep of denial and move it into the spotlight.

# BOOK 3

# SIX ELEMENTS OF HEALING

*In 2002, one in every eight rape victims was male.*

—National Crime Victimization Survey (2002)

## CHAPTER 14

# THERAPY OR "TALKING DOCTORS"

For me, as well as for many of us, therapy is the starting point *only* when we find a safe haven—a place where we can disencumber ourselves without fear of speaking openly and freely—can we comprehend why we are the way we are and how we can change to become healthier. Finding the right therapist is crucial, and being open to change and discovery is vital.

\* \* \* \* \* \*

It was only in retrospect and after analyzing the great variety of ways I pursued some level of healing on my own that I realized the **first element** in my healing process began by meeting with a psychologist, or what I call a *talking doctor. By that I mean* a therapist or psychologist who specializes in working with the sexually abused. *Do not do this with anyone who is not supremely qualified in this subject matter.* You don't want to waste your time.

This process provides you with the opportunity to discover what actually goes on inside yourself, maybe for the first time. There may be a huge inner world you have forgotten. If you are already aware of SA, use a facilitator to more fully comprehend your memories of what you went through. Beyond sexual abuse, the purpose of therapy is to assist you in overcoming problems, whether they involve relationships, behaviors, phobias, beliefs, thoughts and/or emotions. Your personal support system is incredibly important as well. As one psychiatrist wrote, "Having a good friend and discussing one's problems is worth at least three therapy sessions."

Regarding my own SA circumstances, it was definitely seeing a "talking therapist" that allowed me to begin exploring my inner dimensions and subconscious. It also unlocked horrible memories of my past SA I had successfully, consciously blocked out. You may question if there is truly a benefit for unleashing such memories, but, as I came to understand they were still playing havoc with my daily thoughts, feelings, behaviors, and giving me a regularity of nightmares. Remembering them and bringing them into the light was really my *only* hope for a healing to take place.

Unfortunately, this is also where I wasted much time, energy, and money. Unable to move beyond my SA discoveries with the first therapist with whom I discovered these hidden memories, I went from new therapist to new therapist always looking for the elusive actual and real healing. Unfortunately, I discovered no therapist knew where to take me— what path for me to follow to heal.

If we all have biases, this certainly is one of mine: it is my strong belief that, to continue working with *talking therapists* who do not have the knowledge/experience/techniques to help further our healing, we need to stop and find a new course of action. I spent thousands of dollars and multiple hours with therapists who provided very little additional help.

This frustrating dilemma eventually led me to discover some of the most recent and revelatory methods for helping sexual abuse, rape, and domestic violence victims. I may have wasted some twenty-five years, but this new area of discovery transported me into a whole new arena of hope: EMDR became a key feature in my recovery.

*Whereas 93% of juvenile sexual assault victims
knew their attacker, 34.2% were family members,
57.8% were acquaintances, only 7% were strangers.*

—RAINN ((Rape, Abuse & Incest National Network)

CHAPTER 15

# THREE NEW PSYCHOLOGICAL TECHNIQUES

There were not many alternative healing methods for SA victims, especially when I began my search. As a therapist, if the patient is not getting any better, they need to cease treatment and stop taking their money. It seems dishonest to me. And, you as a client need to search for someone who can help you achieve what works to make you feel in control.

Why *none* of the many therapists I had worked with ever suggested we try some new techniques to contribute to my healing, I can only speculate. It took many years of searching blindly before I stumbled upon the first and most beneficial of the three therapies listed below. It was EMDR that catapulted me into finding my **second element** of healing:

➤ EMDR (Eye Movement Desensitization and Reprocessing)

This was the next huge step in my healing process. I realize EMDR, at the time, was a relatively new technique and its effectiveness was often downplayed by therapists.

The great thing about EMDR is that you do not have to understand how it works to benefit from it. It works for some and not for others. Another benefit is you'll find out immediately if it's right for you—it does not require long-term therapy. If you have one traumatic event, the EMDR will be effective more quickly than had there been multiple events. It took me longer because of the prevalence of incidents by my father. But it did work for me.

Developed by Dr. Francine Shapiro, its genesis came one day as she was strolling through a park. Especially stressed that day, she became aware that, when a troubling thought appeared in her mind, her eyes would move rapidly from side to side. She also recognized that, after these eye movements occurred, the intensity of the negative feelings associated with the thought *decreased.*

A certified EMDR therapist, Leslie Goth, in Broomfield, Colorado, provided a more technical understanding of why EMDR works. "It works because eye movements mimic REM sleep (the brain's attempts, when we're dreaming, to process unprocessed information), which creates bi-lateral stimulation in the brain. This bi-lateral stimulation in the brain connects to the amygdala (the part of the brain which retains our emotions) and helps "unstick" the unprocessed memories and body sensations that are tied to the traumas. It is from our amygdala that we have our PTSD reactions and responses to certain stimuli. [I learned from her that talk therapy does not and cannot reach the amygdala], which is why the bi-lateral stimulation is so effective and why real healing can happen via EMDR therapy."

I did not initially have this level of understanding. For me, it worked; I felt it; and somehow knew it.

This simple, noninvasive technique proved so effective for me that, after my first session with the EMDR Consultant in Greenwood Village,

Colorado, after arriving feeling low, depressed, and lethargic, I left in noticeably better spirits. Soon thereafter, following other EMDR sessions, I sensed the glimmer of something in myself never before perceived—value. For the first time, perhaps in my whole life, I realized I might have actual worth.

## HOW EMDR WORKS
### FROM A *LAYPERSON'S* PERSPECTIVE

*This is what I remembered and what worked for me. I know there are derivations used by different EMDR therapists and that some EMDR Therapists have informed me that incorrect protocol was used in my therapy. Regardless, the fact remains that the EMDR Therapy still worked and changed my life.*

That said, working with a therapist trained in EMDR is very, very important—perhaps that you should even be so bold as to inquire how long the therapist has worked with EMDR, how often they use it in their practice and their success rates.

At my EMDR session, I was told to recall a painful or unwanted feeling that came with a memory. Next, I allowed myself to fully immerse into the feeling—that is, recall the past negative feelings as if I were experiencing it in the present. Then, the therapist began moving her hand from side to side in front of my face while my eyes followed. During this process, she would repeat a phrase that best described my feeling, a phrase with wording the two of us had agreed on.

As simple as it sounds, within seconds I could no longer *hold onto* the feeling—it diminished. Said differently, perhaps my mind reprogrammed the feeling's intensity out of my memory.

I had many, many incidences of sexual and emotional abuse, and the process worked for each feeling we identified at the time. Because of the large number of incidents, it did take a while to process through them.

Let me be more specific.

Let's say the unwanted feeling could be stated this way: "Because of all the degrading ways my father treated me, I felt like the lowest form of scum possible." Then, while watching the therapist move her finger back and forth as she repeated this statement, I found, after five or ten seconds, the eye movements greatly diminished the intensity of that emotion to the point it had little negative effect for me. (It did not totally eliminate the feeling or the memory, but diminished the intensity of the emotion.)

I must confess these sessions evoked weird bodily and mental responses from me: My body often jumped involuntarily and often quite violently; sometimes I gagged over a trashcan when recalling some of the most obscene SA experiences. However, the most frightening of all came when another personality emerged and took over complete control of my body and mind. This occurred twice and scared me to death because I was afraid, both times, that I wouldn't be able to regain control of the real me and because, afterwards, I kept recalling the old movie, *Three Faces of Eve*, which depicted a lady with three different personalities. Fortunately, the other personality did depart prior to the end of each session. Scared out of my wits over this rather radical new twist, both Ms. Marzano (the EMDR therapist I was working with) and a psychiatrist conferred with each other and both assured me this was not so abnormal, considering the severity of abuse I had endured.

Other bizarre effects from dredging the bottom

of the barrel of my darkest memories included three unsuccessful suicide attempts; two in the bathroom with a knife; the other much earlier with a gun in my mouth sitting in the closet (all took place during the EMDR therapy). Another memory that surfaced in that zone happened sometimes just before going to sleep. I would start screaming; then, just as suddenly, I would fall into a deep sleep. However, one of the strangest experiences was when, in the middle of a dream, I suddenly became conscious that I was dreaming and heard some other entity within the dream say very distinctly, "We made a mistake. This is too hard for him." I have never figured out the source of the voice nor have I ever heard it again.

During the EMDR, Ms. Marzano said she could actually see the physiological change in my face— my facial expression shifted from pain to calmness. I was also told my fast reaction shift was not far from the norm. In fact, one in three patients experienced immediate, dramatic effects. Some patients require more time for various reasons.

I vaguely recalled watching Barbara Walters, on the television news magazine *20/20* some ten to fifteen years ago, who said that "EMDR is a novel form of therapy ... amazing ... a miracle though it may seem."

I want to make a disclaimer note to the following other potential methods as I did not experience them myself. What I can attest to is that EMDR definitely worked for me and affected me deeply.

\* \* \* \* \* \*

Another healing method I came across but did not personally use is *similar to EMDR*. It also involves recalling bad experiences. Instead of moving a finger back and forth in front the patient's face, the therapist has the individual describe the situation in story format. Then, together, they would create a new, healthier story that would over-power the original story. Through repeated telling of the new story, soon it dominated the old story and became a permanent new memory, thus eliminating or reducing the credibility of the old story. Ergo, the new story takes the old story's place in the mind's memory. You may have heard the expression, "All we are is the stories we tell ourselves." This approach motivates us to *write new stories.*

216

It's like when you have just completed knitting a new sweater; after trying it on, you discover it is too small. Then, rather than throwing it all away, you unravel the yarn and follow with *reweaving* it so the size of the sweater is now larger.

This practice seems credible for me as I recall reading a newspaper article ten years or so ago. It involved the discovery of a small race of natives, I think, deep in the jungle in the Philippines. What was so unusual about this tribe was, first, they had had no interaction with any other race of people, and second, the visiting sociologists discovered this society had no violence.

In trying to discern how this could be possible, they found no evidence as to why ... except that every morning the tribe would gather around and share alarming dreams any of members had experienced the previous night. For any of these dreams that were frightening, the individual who had the dream would counteract the fear in the dream with a new story where they became more powerful and strong. For example, if the dreaming individual was being chased by a ferocious tiger, the new story would have him/her become a fierce warrior and kill the tiger with a spear.

\* \* \* \* \* \*

The third technique involves combining the practices of Neuro-Linguistic Programming, (NLP) and Hypnotism. NLP claims there is a connection between "neuro" (neurological processes of the brain and spinal cord), linguistic, or language, and programming (behavior patterns learned through experience. I have not personally tried this method, but I have heard from others it has proven to be very effective.

For me, all these techniques disclosed the malleability and power of the brain, characteristics that enable us to *rewrite* those life stories that proved to be too frightening to cope with and were negatively affecting our lives. Fortunately, I discovered the veracity of this statement and proved it to be true in my own life.

*If a rape is reported to the police, there is only a 50.8% chance that an arrest will be made.*

—NCPA from the Dept. of Justice statistics and RAINN, NCVS 2002 & UCR

## CHAPTER 16

# PLAYING THE VICTIM

Strangely enough, the **third element** that contributed to my healing came about from eventually and clearly comprehending that our society seems to be obsessed and enmeshed in a culture of *victimhood*. Daily newscasts exemplify this. It seems we are a people competing for status as either victims or defenders of victims. The irony is that those sexually abused are *true victims* when you describe a victim as someone who has been treated unfairly.

Unfortunately, but no less importantly, the process of healing *requires* one to move out of the victim role and claim a strength that may be secretly hiding within. The nature of the beast requires us to shed the underlying feelings of helplessness and seek the natural power residing within us. Like the mystic, Meister Eckhart, wrote back in the thirteenth century: "Every living thing is born with a *funklein* (a spark of divinity) within; and during their life they can fan that spark and make it larger, or they can ignore it. But the most fascinating thing is that the spark never goes out!" If it helps, put a sign on your refrigerator: FAN THE SPARK!

It is so important for every abuse victim to be able to dispel and release any and all vestiges of being a victim, and claim your inner strength.

What proved to be interesting was the fact that, for most of my life, I was in total denial that I had even been playing this role. It wasn't until I attended a week-long seminar that I discovered this weakness. It was the facilitator who actually informed me, and I can still feel the rage and disbelief I felt towards this lady. The audacity of her! Why? Because I am a big, muscular, tough guy who strongly held the belief that victims are wimpy, spineless people!

By the end of the week, and for the first time in my life journey, I finally glimpsed (with growing credibility) the reality that my life was ensconced in playing the abhorrent role of victimhood. This little breakthrough expanded, disclosing parts of me that were shameful, yet, eventually, became beneficial. By being aware, I had the choice of recognizing there was another reality possible for me. Simply put, I now had the choice to change, even though I didn't know how to accomplish this.

It's like a psychological cartoon of a person walking on the street. Upon coming to a large hole in the street the first time, the person falls into the hole. The second time, the same thing happens, along with the third and fourth times. But, finally, the person becomes aware of the hole in the street and chooses to walk around it. It's the same thing with the adversities or negative events in our lives; we can keep doing them or we can choose a better life.

In our lives, the role of victimhood is portrayed so frequently, and when we recognize it, we have the choice of not falling into it and experiencing all the injuries and pain. Now, we can choose to walk around it.

Please note that something does happen when someone is playing the victim role that effects their whole being; and the same is true for when we are able to break out of that formerly weak role to one of recapturing one's strengths. There is no doubt that each of us is doing the best we can with the knowledge we have. So when we are exposed to other information and gain an awareness of the roles we have been playing, great new possibilities become attainable.

This recognition came hard for me and was embarrassing to admit to someone else. But, like the other two elements, this **third step** proved extremely important in my recovery.

*About four out of ten sexual assaults*
*take place at the victims' home.*

—Sex Offenses and Offenders, Bureau of Justice
Statistics, U.S. Dept. of Justice, February 1997

## CHAPTER 17

# OVERCOMING ADDICTIONS

If you are fearful about having to stop your addiction/addictions—these creative mechanisms you utilized as a means of coping, these actions that allowed you to stay alive—then focus, instead, on how your addictions "benefited" you. Then, if you want to find a better way to deal with the effects of having been sexually abused and halt your past destructive choices (i.e., the only ones you knew to use at the time), you can choose new ones that are now available to you. Replacing your addictions with better and healthier coping mechanisms allows you to enter a whole new world.

For me, it began with attending AA, Alcoholic

Anonymous and NA, Narcotics Anonymous. Never in my wildest imagination could I ever have conceived becoming a member of this organization. The only contacts I had with it were from a few people I had known who praised it so often and spoke of its benefits so frequently I sometimes feared I would throw up a little in my mouth. Yes, the AA members I knew made me hate this organization before I even knew anything about it.

It took me two to three years of intermittently attending meetings to discover what it was really about and how it worked and before my defense mechanisms and rationalizations lowered enough for me to clearly see its benefits. Here are a few important facts:

> At first, it really frustrated me when these idiots kept repeating every time they spoke in a meeting—"Hi, I'm John Doe and I'm an alcoholic." I mean, why in the hell did they have to repeat it so often? Didn't they already know they were an alcoholic?

I came to understand that alcoholism is a disease of denial, meaning that not only do you deny you

228

are one at first, but this denial can pop up at any time even after you've stopped drinking, regardless of how long you've been sober. I was shocked to hear people who were legally bound to attend meetings by the courts. They continued to proclaim they were not alcoholics despite three or four DWIs (Driving While Intoxicated), multiple trips to the Emergency Room for alcohol poisoning and losing their families, homes, and jobs because of their drinking.

I also heard sad, sad stories of people who had been sober for decades. They suddenly questioned if they were still alcoholics and began drinking again, only to discover that alcoholism is a progressive disease that never goes away. Like herpes, alcoholism is forever; just one drink and they found themselves again caught up in the addiction and not able to stop.

> I learned that alcoholism is truly a disease and was classified as one by the American Medical Association back in the 1950s.

> No one can convince another person to stop drinking if they are an alcoholic; not a wife or husband, boss, or one's children. Only the alcoholic person can do this.

➢ There are two aspects involved with alcoholism: the first is the obvious *physical addiction*, which is the body's craving for it and withdrawal effects when denied alcohol. It's a condition where you believe you can have just one drink ... until the alcohol hits your system, and then the craving kicks in and you find yourself unable to stop.

Then, there is the *mental obsession*, which is actually the most difficult to break. By mental obsession, I mean how your mind becomes obsessed with the thought of drinking alcohol, i.e., you wake up in the morning and plan with what food and the places and times you will drink alcohol. While driving, you pass a liquor store and imagine seeing a blinking neon sign in front of the store with your name on it, inviting you to come in. Or, you pass a bar that you frequented, and you automatically turn into the parking lot. This is the mental element part of addiction.

➢ You could come to believe there is no earthly power that will help you stop drinking.

However, perhaps with time, you will discover a power that will help you.

➢ You will see a lot of weird people in AA. You will recognize these people are a bit strange because they haven't emotionally matured, meaning their emotional development was arrested when they began excessive drinking. You may recognize your own "weirdness," especially when you first begin, as I did.

➢ If you wonder what can help you stop drinking or abusing drugs, you may want to start attending AA/NA meetings to discover some answers.

I even tried a 30-day rehab program that taught me a lot about alcoholism, kept me sober for 30 days plus an additional 42 days after leaving, and was definitely beneficial, but I still began drinking again after 72 days. It was in AA meetings where I learned that "Rehab is for self-disclosure, AA is for recovery."

Without a doubt, for me to stop using alcohol— my last and most persistent drug of choice—would not have been possible without the AA Program. Before this, I believed I could not cope with my world without alcohol and drugs. However, I came to understand that these coping mechanisms kept me alive at first. But, somewhere along the way, *they* became a definite hindrance to my wellbeing.

Other options beyond AA that also had good results include SMART Recovery, HAMS, Moderation Management, Women for Sobriety, SOS, LifeRing, and Rational Recovery. The key is to find the one that works best for you and stick with it.

Eventually, along your healing journey, you, too, *will* come to see—to understand what I finally realized— that, every time I drank excessively or partook of some drug, I perpetuated my "victimhood." I know this may be difficult to understand at first, but while these drugs initially kept me alive, they were also killing me; and only a victim would allow themselves to be so harmed through ingesting the drugs.

AA or NA can work for you ... if you are ready for a better life ... when you are sick and tired of being sick and tired. However, if you are not ready to quit, don't waste your time nor expect to heal from your abuses. Trying and failing is normal as long as you keep trying. I promise you there is a great, great life awaiting you. Don't quit before the miracle happens.

*If an arrest for sexual assault is made, there is an 80% chance of prosecution. If there is a prosecution, there is only a 58% chance of a felony conviction— most are given a simple misdemeanor conviction.*

—NCPA from us Dept. of Justice statistics and
RAINN, NCVS 2000 & UCR

CHAPTER 18

# THE PURPOSE OF ALL ADVERSITIES

*Every person must walk through their fire alone.*
*That is what gives them their strength and character.*

—Maxwell Winston Stone,
*Chipped But Not Broken*

I want to emphasize the importance of that quote by Albert Einstein I cited earlier: "One of the greatest secrets in all the world ... is that every adversity brings with it a gift."

I still recall becoming quite upset and angry the first time I read his idea. How in the hell could someone with his brains make such a blanket and ignorant statement, especially if he didn't know the pain of being a sexual abuse survivor? Only a short while later, however, I realized the statement's validity.

Only after overcoming my blindness over Einstein's words, only after searching for just what gift could have derived from my SA, only after opening to its possibility was I finally able to see it. Most likely, the gift will be different for each of us, but, no doubt about it, it is there waiting to be discovered—for all of us.

"Synchronicity" is a beautiful word to me, which means "when an event happens that, at first, you thought to be totally random, only to later grasp the truth that it wasn't a random act at all but somehow, maybe, had been planned all along." Suddenly, I began finding synchronous quotes and stories in my everyday affairs.

One story I happened upon compared someone's real life and the difficult things they had gone through with the process a blacksmith used in creating a new shape of metal. First, in the process of making a new tool, the blacksmith pumps the bellows to raise the temperature of the furnace fire. Then, he places a bit of iron on the fire until it heats up and achieves a kind of translucent, glass-like state. Next, he removes it from the fire, places it on an anvil, and with it in its pliable state, he is now able to pound the iron with a heavy hammer into a new, different shape than it originally held. Finally, the blacksmith thrusts the hot metal into cold water so the dramatic temperature change *tempers* the metal, making it harder and stronger than before.

From this little anecdotal story (see my book entitled *Chipped But Not Broken*), I saw this was just like life: our adversities heat us up; we are beat around; and then thrust into situations we were not expecting, which make us stronger. Furthermore, I glimpsed this was, perhaps, the way the human spirit is formed, developed, and then strengthened. This was not easy to see at first, but soon, the little light bulb came on clearly, lighting my way to a new insight.

Throughout history, it seems every person, great or small, has a background of adversity. I read about Martin Luther King becoming great only after being arrested many times for leading peace marches and trying to help all races see their oneness; the same for Mahatma Gandhi, who became great only after he was thrown off a train for the color of his skin; Helen Keller discovered her greatness only after overcoming the incredible limitations of being blind and deaf; Abraham Lincoln's number of failed elections are legendary, and he had to overcome devastating depression to become President of the United States; and Franklin Delano Roosevelt's strength in rising above the crippling, emotional, and physically debilitating effects of polio has been attributed to his later success in his own presidency.

I came to envision, to grasp that my personal adversities might even have been preordained, preselected for me to experience to accelerate my abilities and talents; none of which would probably have been developed had it not been for those adversities. I also clearly perceived and, most importantly, came to comprehend it was those adversities that actually made those other people become great. Perhaps, my sexual abuse could and would, somehow, prove to be beneficial to me.

As a kid, did you ever come upon a butterfly struggling to emerge from a cocoon?

If you were lucky enough to observe this fascinating event, your first inclination may have been to help the poor butterfly by cutting open the cocoon with a knife to make its fight to free itself easier. However, if you had done so, you would have contributed to the butterfly's demise.

How? The butterfly needs the struggle because it is the struggle itself that squeezes the blood out of the body and into the wings so it may fly. Without the adversity of the struggle, without all the squeezing and strenuous wriggling, the butterfly would be unable to fly when it emerged and therefore become easy prey for a passing frog or bird.

These metaphors aided my understanding that it is the struggles we go through in life that allow us to fly, to develop our strength and character.

While SA is certainly one of the most arduous, difficult adversities a human has to deal with, what if it turned out not to be the crippling disaster we have always believed it to be but, actually, an event placed in our paths so we could learn to fly higher because of it?

\* \* \* \* \* \*

In Ireland, following the potato famine when economic struggles were the norm of the day, one large Irish family made a big decision.

First, the father decided he had to stop spending so much money drinking in the pubs and begin working at any job, however lowly, whenever he could get them. His four boys would work wherever they could find odd jobs, while the three girls and the mother would sell butter and eggs and do laundry and housekeeping for the richer families. All the money earned was to be pooled for one goal—paying the cost of tickets for passage on a ship that would transport them all to the opportunity-filled United States.

After much hard work, the family finally earned enough money. However, at the ticket office, the proud father discovered they could only afford to purchase nonrefundable tickets for the family. Certain that nothing could stop them from going, he gladly paid. Plans were made to leave their home and board the ship that would sail in two weeks.

Then, the unexpected happened. One of the sons was bitten by a rabid dog. Initially thinking this would be no hindrance to their cherished trip, everything came to a screeching halt when a local veterinarian informed them the lad was required, by law, to be quarantined for four weeks. The family was crushed. Their hard-earned money was lost and all their dreams and hopes of going to America were now utterly destroyed.

The father became bitter and returned to his drinking at the pubs.

One day, however, upon staggering into his favorite pub, he overheard some men discussing the news that a liner going to America had hit an iceberg and sunk causing the deaths of fifteen hundred and two passengers.

Of course, it was Titanic, the very ship on which they had booked their passage.

Putting down his drink, the now thankful father hurried home to tell his family the news. Gathering them all around, the humbled man had everyone get down on their knees and give thanks to God for saving all their lives. What had looked like the greatest tragedy, the worst thing to happen to them turned out to be the very thing that saved their lives!

Have you ever heard of a Stradivarius violin? Perhaps the greatest violin ever made, its wood was harvested from only the toughest forest in Northern

Croatia. This maple wood, known for its extreme density, resulted from slow growth brought about by the harshest winds and weather conditions in the Croatian winters.

Why did the violin maker use such wood? Because only the toughest wood, the wood that had been grown under the most adverse circumstances, could produce the sweetest sounds in the entire world.

*Could this be the same for you and me?*

*So, even in those 39% of rapes reported to police, there is only a 16.3% chance the rapists will end up in prison.*

—NCPA from US Dept. of Justice statistics and RAINN, NCVS 2002 & UCR

## CHAPTER 19

# FORGIVENESS

For me, the last key to healing from SA proved to be another really tough one, for *how can you forgive the person who so harmed you?*

As a minister, ordained and trained who often spoke on the importance of forgiveness, and after rereading all the Biblical quotes and stories on its importance, I found, *none of them worked for me.* In fact, I often vowed there was no way I could ever forgive the son-of-a-bitch who did this to me—my own father.

That is, until after extensive reading and plodding through article after article and book after book on the very elusive act of forgiveness, a radical and rather extreme idea began to emerge from my brain unconsciously synthesizing all that I had read. What emerged represented the sixth and final element in my journey of healing: to forgive the seemingly unforgiveable, all I had to do was devise or create a "story," which I could accept, that explained why my abuser had done what he had done to me.

This is the story my wife and I came up with. We had been speculating in the area of spiritual ideas of reincarnation so we focused on this arena and asked ourselves, "What if, before we came to earth, and still retaining our belief that our Creator gave us free will to do most anything we wanted ... what if we had a *meeting* with our closest friends throughout all eternity and each agreed to play certain roles or parts, like in a play, that would teach each of us whatever it was we came here to earth to learn?

Furthermore, another radical, uncomfortable and even more embarrassing thought emerged: what if, in another life, "I" had been a sexual abuser and chose to be sexually abused in this life to eradicate any further desires that may still be lingering in this area for all eternity. What better way to stop from ever sexually abusing others than to be on the victimized end?

Additionally, what if my father, as a great gift to me, agreed to play this dastardly role?

Of course, in the context of this new story I created, forgiveness became easy, and I rehearsed it in my thinking. No, I did not forgive him for how he treated me here on earth, but I did forgive him, within the spiritual realm, for his great sacrifice he made.

This story I created may seem foolish to you. For me, it totally allowed me to forgive and release the extreme hatred and anger I had been carrying for so long. You see, anger and non-forgiveness affects only the victim, certainly not the perpetrator. It's like the idea of wanting to kill someone by poisoning, but you drink the poison yourself. **Remember:** Forgiveness is for *you*, not for the benefit of the one you are forgiving.

It is also important to know that forgiveness does not mean that the abuser is not held accountable for their actions here on earth. I discovered that I could truly forgive my father and still separate that forgiveness from the actions he performed on me which were unfathomable.

This proved to be the last missing link to recover from sexual abuse and to actually proclaim that I had reached the highest level of healing ever before attained by me; something I had thought would never occur ... something I thought would be a complete impossibility!

To reiterate the sixth element in the healing process—forgiveness—is to simply create any story that allows you to be able to forgive your abuser. This may sound facetious and simplistic, but it really worked for me and, if you have been unable to forgive utilizing the traditional rationale for doing so, perhaps this could work for you, too.

# BOOK 4

# AND FINALLY ...

## CHAPTER 20

# SUMMARIZED STEPS OF HEALING

This summarization clearly delineates the most important steps I took in my healing process. While you may discover or need different things to heal, this is my testimony of what worked for me and just might work for you, too:

> ➢ Work with a "talking therapist," either a therapist, psychotherapist or social worker who has a background dealing with sexual abuse clients;

> ➢ Utilize EMDR or one of the other two techniques discussed and, again, ensure you

work with a trained therapist experienced in this process;

➢ Recognize you've been "playing" a victim role;

➢ Find a way to stop all your addictions. This should now, and in fact can only be possible if you've already decided to get healthy;

➢ Begin pondering the idea that all adversity brings with it a gift, even with sexual abuse, although each person must discover their own unique gifts; and,

➢ Find a way to forgive your perpetrator/ perpetrators.

As Winston Churchill wrote to the people of England during their war with Hitler and the Nazis, "Never give up. Never, never, never, never give up. Never. Never. Never!"

## CHAPTER 21

# RELATIONSHIPS

One of the biggest and most detrimental effects from the SA I experienced was definitely in the area of interpersonal relationships. Starting with dating as a teenager and continuing through with wives and other intimate relationships, and with my children, the unhealthy relationships I participated in were all testimony to my confused, lousy, and poor interrelationship skills that will forever stain me with regret, and continue to haunt me forever. I wish I could go back to *most* of those relationships, *certainly not all, but most,* and try to apologize, not as an excuse but as an explanation to those involved as to why I did such a lousy job. I had crazy role models from whom I learned; I was running scared and was mentally confused; I was governed by internal nightmares that tainted and hid so much of who I really was. There is so very much I wish I could go back and have a "do over."

The real irony is that being a solid and dependable, trusting, warm, giving, and stable family man was my most coveted dream, characteristics I most wanted to represent. Yet, because of my past, because of the darkness, my low self-worth, drug addictions, anger, and seeming-to-be-accident-prone, I was consumed in shame, guilt, and feelings of worthlessness.

As reality dictates that the past is the past, all I can do now is try to do the next best thing and cope with these past rueful memories as well as I can.

\* \* \* \* \* \*

On a much more positive note, since my just recent healing, my life has suddenly become so much easier. I have finally succeeded in a relationship—the one with my wife is simply fabulous. She and I have developed a most loving, safe, and fun environment in our home, and she says I am the most gentle man she has ever been with and feels safer with me than in any other relationship. It has been easier to love her than anyone else, and she has become the most beautiful, kind, giving, and supportive person I have ever known. We are growing to spiritual depths that before, I could only have dreamt to have achieved. And, of course, my emotional and physical health continues improving every day. It seems I have achieved a certain nirvana with an appreciative attitude of living. Yes, grievous past tormenting memories still arise, but they are infrequent, and I deal with them by remembering to feel the pain and then release it. Rather than attempting to numb the pain, I am somehow able to cope quite healthily now, perhaps even like normal people and am living a life that is beyond my dreams.

\* \* \* \* \* \*

Like all long important journeys that end in success, it has been agonizingly difficult. But, for you who now can receive the story that finally brought me healing, *your time schedule will be shortened.* When I first began stumbling around in the dark some thirty-eight years ago, I literally could not find any program or process that worked. There were probably other survivors who had found the right combination of healing elements that worked for them. This one simply worked for me ... and it could work for you.

*Adversity introduces a person to themselves.*

—Epictetus (AD 55-AD 135),
Roman Sage and Philosopher

---

*The soul would have no rainbow*
*had the eyes no tears.*

—John Vance Cheney (1848-1922),
American Poet, Essayist, and Librarian

## Chapter 22

# Hope

Joseph Campbell wrote a book called *The Hero with a Thousand Faces*. In it, he disclosed a rather profound discovery: **there is a hero within everyone's life journey.**

He revealed this truth by comparing each of our lives to the mythical storytelling that has taken place since the beginning of time. After reading the greatest mythological stories expounded throughout history, Joseph Campbell was able to see that a pattern existed from which each of our own individual lives closely followed.

Joseph Campbell's book was then followed by a seemingly simple little memo, which turned into the now-legendary 7-page Memo. This short document, authored by Christopher Vogler, a Hollywood screenwriter who then worked for the Disney company, resulted in Vogler's book, *The Writer's Journey: Mythic Structures for Storytellers and Screenwriters.*

Basically, what is most important for every sexually abused person is that both men, Campbell and Vogler, identified that there is a pattern adhered to by every great drama, storytelling, myth, and religious ritual that has ever been told and passed down from generation to generation. Furthermore, this pattern or stages that each hero in a story goes through during their lifetime is actually the same stages each of us can go through in our own lives. Whether you are Princess Leia or Luke Skywalker from *Star Wars*, King Arthur, Helen Keller, or President Abraham Lincoln, the point is *each of you* went through similar stages or patterns in your own lives like heroes everywhere.

As sexual abuse survivors, we were born into a life; then there was the call to adventure (obviously, a horrible adventure). At first, the possibility of ever healing seemed too difficult; then, you met a mentor or helper who contributed to you facing your greatest fear—your abuser; and seeing the possibility that healing just might be attainable.

Next, you had to deal with the naysayers who denied your truth of being sexually abused. This resulted in you standing behind your claims and rising out of the ashes of depression, nightmares, and blackness, that had pervaded your life until, finally, you grasped the possibility of healing and were *reborn* after starting the healing steps that were needed. From here, you emerged into wholeness, perhaps for the first time, into health and wholeness rather than the former futility you had felt.

Do you see this? Can you grasp it?

**The hero's journey is your journey. You are the hero in your own life, and you, too, can heal. Your spirit has not dimmed. You are a light in this world and you are needed here.**

# If You Ever

If you ever need to know, you will.

If you ever feel, don't flee.

If you ever hurt, release it. If you ever fly, soar.

If you ever cry, embrace it.

If you ever smile, pass it on.

If you ever die, know you have lived.

If you ever sin, don't sweat it.

If you ever love, give up hate.

If you ever hate, it's a slow death.

If you ever hug, repeat often.

If you ever make love, keep it up.

If you ever take walks, try skipping.

If you ever receive, give back.

If you are ever served, tip heavily.

If you ever feel rich, give even more.

If you ever stumble, know you are not alone.

If you ever have a true friend, know its rarity.

If you ever considered trying, you just might.

If you ever thought you could, you can.

If you ever believe you can,

It's already done!

Eat Lots. Laugh Often. Live Fully.

—Ernie Carwile

# Other Endorsements

"A story of pain I have heard too often. A story of healing that keeps me going. A story of hope for the 60 million Americans who understand. An articulate and very personal account of a major failing in our society and the steps toward health.

— **Michael Elder, LMFT** (licensed marriage and family therapist), Certified EMDR Therapist, CTTS (Certified Trauma Treatment Specialist).

"This is a must read for people dealing with Sexual Abuse (SA), as a client, as a therapist, or BOTH. Ernie shares his more than 60-year painful, but glorious, journey as a victim, addict, suicide attempt, depression, anxiety, and anger. His heroic healing experience is eclectic, including Eye Movement Desensitization and Reprocessing (EMDR) as a pivotal component of his journey. He tells his story with exquisite sensitivity, making it clear why Even the Trees Were Crying. Thank you Ernie for this gift."

— **Richard Murphy Jr., PhD**, Clinical Psychologist, Charter Member EMDRIA, EMDRIA Approved Consultant and Institute Facilitator

"One of the most poignant and heart-rending stories of the atrocities that sexual abuse and incest renders in the lives of its survivors. It is a story of courage, determination and fortitude that rends the veil of secrecy for men and creates hope that healing and restoration is possible."

**—Wanda K. Holloway, PsyD, LPC, LCSW,**
EMDR Certified and Approved Consultant

\* \* \* \* \* \*

I would like to hear from you ... to have you share your story. You can email me at authorcarwile@gmail.com.

Do let me know if you wish your story be kept confidential. I'm certain others will benefit from hearing it.

Your friend, Ernie Carwile

## About the Author

Ernie Carwile was born in Munich, Germany and has lived throughout the world. He is a graduate of the University of Missouri with a B.S. in Business and Finance and the Iliff School of Theology in Denver, Colorado with a Master's Degree.

After high school he sold cemetery plots door-to-door in Hannibal, Missouri, and while attending college, he drove trucks for Peabody Coal Mine. Mr. Carwile has been an Air Force Officer, heavyweight boxer and a Methodist and Congregational minister.

As a celebrated author and master storyteller, Carwile has been featured extensively in the national media including *Good Morning America, Inside Edition, CNN, Associated Press, Court TV,*

*Clear Channel Radio,* the *Los Angeles Times* and the *Rocky Mountain News.*

He has published eleven books and received a great review from the most prestigious *Library Journal,* as well as Endorsements/Thank Yous from the President of the United States, twelve U.S. Governors and such prominent collegiate football coaches as Steve Spurrier.

They also have been translated into five foreign languages.

He and his wife, award-winning author and speaker Mary Catherine Carwile, recently moved to the Phoenix area after living 40 years in Colorado.

P.S. They love it there even more than Colorado!

www.ingramcontent.com/pod-product-compliance
Lightning Source LLC
Chambersburg PA
CBHW051817090426
42736CB00011B/1516